MONETARY RECONSTRUCTION

BY THE SAME AUTHOR

CURRENCY AND CREDIT

8vo, 15s. net

LONGMANS, GREEN AND CO.
London, New York, Toronto, Bombay, Calcutta and Madras

MONETARY
RECONSTRUCTION

BY

R. G. HAWTREY

AUTHOR OF "CURRENCY AND CREDIT"

LONGMANS, GREEN AND CO.

39 PATERNOSTER ROW, LONDON, E.C. 4

NEW YORK, TORONTO

BOMBAY, CALCUTTA AND MADRAS

1923

Made in Great Britain

PREFACE.

OF the essays which form this book, No. III (the Gold Standard) appeared in the "Economic Journal" for December, 1919, and No. VI (the Genoa Resolutions on Currency) in the same periodical for September, 1922. No. IV (the European Currency Situation) appeared in a French translation in the special economic number of the "Revue de Métaphysique et de Morale" for July, 1921. No. V (the Federal Reserve System of the United States) was read to the Royal Statistical Society in February, 1922, and appeared in the Society's Journal. I have to thank the editorial authorities in each case for consenting to republication.

The Introduction and the first two essays appear for the first time.

It has been thought desirable to print the essays in their original form.[1] To test the application of a theory to practical problems, it is better to view the problems and the theory as they appeared at the time than to be wise after the event. It is possible to be highly scientific in *post mortem* investigation, without being very trustworthy in diagnosis or prescription.

In place of a revision of the text, the Introduction supplies comment, and links each essay to the present time. Some of the hopes, fears, and expectations expressed in the essays have not been substantiated, but if the reader will forgive these errors, he will also find, as he passes from case to case, that the diagnosis has

---

[1] One or two superfluous passages have been omitted. In No. V some more recent figures not previously available have been utilised.

sometimes been confirmed by experience, and I trust he may be persuaded to give some measure of assent to the treatment prescribed.

Throughout it has been my aim, in face of a too prevalent scepticism, to show that treatment is possible, that remedies for our present disorders, difficult though they may be to apply, are not beyond human power. In particular I have sought to throw into relief the importance and also the feasibility of a rational control of credit.

R. G. HAWTREY.

November, 1922.

CONTENTS.

INTRODUCTION.

I.

THE six essays which follow have been written at various dates in the last seven years, a period into which have been compressed greater monetary events than might have been expected from seven generations. Each essay belongs to its own time, and relates to the situation as it then appeared. There are some advantages in looking back on the successive phases of our monetary problem in this way, rather than considering it exclusively from the point of view of a present which will itself become a past.

It is the purpose of this introduction to give unity to the collection, by recalling the circumstances at the dates successively dealt with, and by bridging the intervals which separate them.

Essay No. I may appear to have intruded into the volume under false pretences. It is entitled " The Fall in the American Exchange." But it has nothing to do with the falls which have occurred since the war, in 1919, in 1920, or in 1921. It was written in September, 1915, when the question of monetary reconstruction had not risen above the horizon.

The growth of monetary inflation during the war is by now a well-worn theme. This essay of 1915, however, departs so far from the beaten track as to argue that the inflation could have been prevented, or at any rate kept in control, by means of a high bank rate. The argument is of no more than academic interest now, for the circumstances of 1915 can never be exactly repeated. But it raises questions of principle, which have their present application.

At the outbreak of war the foreign exchange market was, as we all know, paralysed. When the first stiff movements of its muscles began in August and September, 1914, most of the neutral exchanges quoted sterling at a substantial premium. Particularly was this true of New York, where sterling was quoted for some time at $5 or little less.

But soon the premium began to dwindle. By the beginning of 1915 the American exchange had fallen to par. By the 1st August, 1915, it had fallen to 4·76, and was thus at a discount of more than 2 per cent. Under peace conditions the exchange could not fall below 4·84 without attracting gold, but difficulties of insurance and transit in war-time widened the gaps between the gold points, and this figure of 4·76 might still be regarded as within the legitimate limits of variation.

But the month of August, 1915, saw something like an exchange panic. The exchange actually fell on one day to 4·50, and only recovered because official support was given in the market, and it became known that gold was soon to arrive from Europe.

The question then arose, what measures could be taken to maintain the exchange. If among the remedies discussed at the time a rise in the bank rate hardly took a serious place, that was because the virtue of a high bank rate had come to be regarded as lying only in its power of attracting short-term loans from abroad, a power which was easily nullified by the expectation of a slight adverse movement of the exchange. It was admitted, no doubt, that dear money had a repressive influence upon business, but this was commonly regarded as something quite separate from its remedial effects, or rather as a drawback to be set against those effects. Little recognition was to be found in financial circles for the view of the bank rate as an instrument for regulating the supply of the means of payment, and therefore for checking inflation.

In the first twelve months of war, money was "cheap." The scorpions of 10 per cent., imposed on the 1st August, 1914, lasted only five days. The mild chastisement of 6 per cent. gave place after two days more to the gentle pressure of 5, and even 5 per cent. was not made effective. In September, 1914, the discount market, then just returning to consciousness, quoted 3 per cent., and in the early part of 1915 the market rate fell below 2. Steps were then taken, it is true, to remedy so extreme and artificial a depression of the discount rate. In March, 1915, the Bank of England began to borrow from the money market, and in April was started the practice of keeping Treasury Bills continuously on offer, and selling them in unlimited quantities at a fixed rate. But the fixed rate remained low till after the issue of the great 4½ per cent. war loan in June and July, 1915 ; it was not raised even to the point required to make a 5 per cent. bank rate effective till August.

The policy of cheap money looked plausible enough. It stimulated trade, and enabled the Government to borrow by means of Treasury bills at small cost. But cheap money stimulates trade because it encourages trade borrowing; it increases production because it accelerates consumption. Its advantages in the circumstances of 1915 were utterly deceptive. To prepare the way for war loans by cheap discount rates is to encourage those trade demands for capital which are their most formidable competitors in the investment market.[1] It is like trying to dry a lump of ice by the fire.

This applies to artificially cheap money, that is to say, to the policy of making the discount rate lower than is really appropriate to the state of the market. To gain the real advantages, in the pursuit of which cheap money is advocated, it is necessary to affect the state of the market, and to make the borrowing of money less attractive to traders.

The theory of discount policy is full of paradoxes. Cheap money quickly swells trade profits and leads to dear money. Once this has begun, the only way back to cheap money is through a regime of dearer money still. This has never been better exemplified than in the last three years. In the present year, 1922, for the first time since the outbreak of war in 1914, the investment market has been favourable to borrowers. That is simply the natural sequel of a severe regime of 7 per cent. and deflation.

It may be argued that conditions are not the same in war-time. But, as is contended in the essay, that part of the business of the country which caters for private consumption

---

[1] See " Currency and Credit," pp. 93-4.

is just as sensitive to credit policy as in peace time. Private consumption competes under war conditions with the Government in its demands upon the country's productive resources, and sets the standard of prices, of wages, and of profits. If inflation of prices and wages is to be prevented, or at any rate to be checked, private consumption must be kept within limits. High taxation and the encouragement of savings will work towards this effect, but may be completely defeated if once the vicious circle of inflation is started. The ideal of raising all the funds required for such a war as that of 1914 by taxation and genuine investment may have been unattainable. But it is difficult to avoid the conclusion that, if in the opening months of the war the 5 per cent. bank rate had been made rigorously effective, still more if the rate had been put up to 6 or 7 per cent. for long enough to initiate a credit contraction, all the operations of war finance would have been enormously facilitated. The yield of taxation would not have grown so quickly (in terms of paper pounds), but neither would the prices of commodities. And the investment market would have been immensely strengthened.

But in 1915 people did not believe in the bank rate. In the course of seventy years' successful experience, the control of credit by means of the bank rate had become a piece of routine. Just because it worked smoothly, it was not the subject of controversy, and because it was not the subject of controversy, the theory underlying it was neglected.

We are still suffering from the prevalence of scepticism on this vital question, and there is always a danger that action may be delayed thereby at a critical moment. The intimate dependence of the regulation of a monetary system upon credit control is a theme to which we shall return presently (see especially V and VI below).

If it is argued here that credit control through the bank rate is practicable and desirable, even under war conditions, that must not be taken to mean that the system can never lose its virtue. When a currency has reached a state of extreme discredit, through the resort to recklessly inflationary finance, trade borrowing dwindles towards vanishing point for sheer want of a trustworthy unit of account (see No. IV). It is then and only then that the discount rate ceases to be a factor in the problem.

II.

No. II, which deals with "Inflation," was written in September, 1916. But though written in the middle of the war, it is concerned not with war finance but with after-war conditions. It is in the nature of a forecast of the transition from war to peace.

In 1916 the American exchange was pegged. Since the issue of the Anglo-French loan of $500 millions in New York in October, 1915, every effort had been devoted to the provision of assets in America, both for the payment of the Government's dollar liabilities, and for the sale of exchange to traders. Not only were loans issued, but gold was sent, and dollar securities were collected in England and sold in America.

The process of inflation, which had already been in full swing in 1915, was growing apace. The index of wholesale prices had been 25 per cent. above the pre-war standard in September, 1915 ; it was 60 per cent. above it in September, 1916. But by that time inflation had spread to the United States. American prices, which were still at the pre-war level in September, 1915, had risen 30 per cent. in September, 1916, and were rising rapidly. If they were still relatively so much lower than English prices, that was partly perhaps because some relative fall in American prices was in any case due after the reduction of the tariff in 1913, but still more because the obstruction to imports into England and other belligerent countries on private account, owing to war conditions, had the same effect as a protective tariff against American products.

Even the obstruction of imports did not prevent the exchanges recording a discount on sterling. The pegging measures kept the discount in New York down to about 2 per cent. But at some neutral centres it was substantially higher. Gold movements, apart from those initiated under Government auspices, were in almost complete abeyance. What was to happen on the removal of war restrictions, when all this pent-up inflation would be given its full effect? That is the subject of this second essay.

Tremendous events were to pass before the moment came. In the realm of war finance the entry of the United States into the war in April, 1917, stands foremost. By it the pegging of the exchange was greatly facilitated. Not only were dollars advanced by the United States Government to provide for our purchases in America, but in America itself the expedients of war finance intensified the inflation which had already begun. American prices rose rapidly. In September, 1917, the export of gold from America was prohibited, and in a short time the principal neutral currencies were quoted at high premiums in New York.

But for all that the situation in March, 1919, when the pegging of the exchanges ceased, was not fundamentally different from that which it was possible to foresee in 1916. Inflation, great as it was in the United States, was greater still here. The demands of trade for more capital, fixed and circulating, began to be felt. They were felt in America too, but not with the same intensity.

For the moment in both countries there was a pause. Every one expected that the advent of peace would mean a fall of prices, and the expectation itself tended to bring about the fall. Nevertheless the return of peace conditions, and the unpegging of the exchanges, threatened an immediate export of gold from England on a huge scale, and the export of gold was accordingly prohibited.

This measure was not in essence a change. It only prolonged by enactment a restriction which had long been imposed by circumstances. But it left credit free to expand further. If gold movements had become free, specie payments being maintained,[1] a contraction of credit would have been necessary to protect the country's gold reserves. As it was, credit expanded and inflation grew without hindrance, till the advance of the bank rate to 7 per cent. in April, 1920 (the earlier

---

[1] Either measure without the other would have been insufficient. Specie payments have been maintained without a break during and since the war.

advance to 6 per cent. in November, 1919, having had no visible effect). Prices rose far above the war-time level, bank advances increased, trade displayed an unhealthy feverish activity.

Whether this inflation was preventable or not, there is likely to be general agreement that its effects were on the whole deplorable. In the light of subsequent experience the estimate made in the essay of 1916 as to the relative importance of its ill effects certainly requires revision. " That the continuance of inflation means the continuance and indeed enhancement of war prices after the conclusion of peace is in itself only a minor disadvantage," or again, " there would be some hardship and injustice, but hardly so great as to be a conclusive argument against continued inflation " (II, p. 40), these are propositions which would now be disputed. The rise of prices was certainly not a " minor disadvantage."

And on the other hand, we have seen sterling fluctuating wildly, and always at a discount, for more than three years, without the dreaded result of an impairment of London's position as a financial centre (II, pp. 40-2). The panic withdrawal of balances has not occurred. In fact it must be confessed that it seems doubtful whether there is any substance in this last-named danger at all. Probably the foreign balances held at a financial centre are normally no greater than are really needed for current business, and can only be withdrawn gradually as the business itself declines.[1] The withdrawal of funds from Europe by American exporters, which caused an exchange panic in January and February, 1920, and to which reference is made below (IV, p. 71, and V, p. 105), was not a case in point, because these funds were really being held as a speculation in exchange.

But it must not be supposed that the financial position of London would in all circumstances be secure against the consequences of a fluctuating currency. In the period since March, 1919, very few countries have possessed a gold standard, and none except the United States[2] have possessed it

---

[1] See " Currency and Credit," pp. 154-6.
[2] Together, perhaps, with Albania and the Hejaz.

continuously. When practically all currencies are varying in relation to one another, traders will look on their variation in relation to the money of a financial centre as a necessary evil. It is only when conditions in other countries are normal, and their currencies stable in relation to one another, that a fluctuating currency becomes a serious handicap.

When a bill is drawn on London by an exporter of goods to Great Britain, he sells the bill to a bank in his own country, and the bank can avoid any appreciable exchange risk by transmitting it immediately to London and getting it discounted there. The importer's liability on the maturity of the bill and the proceeds of sale of the goods are in one and the same currency, sterling, and so he runs no exchange risk.

It is when a bill is drawn on London by an exporter of goods to some other country that the exchange risk arises. For the importer, whose liability to the acceptor on the maturity of the bill is in sterling, will have sold the goods for the currency of his own country. This form of financing is the special characteristic of a great financial centre. If the value of sterling in relation to the foreign currency is variable, there is an exchange risk against which the purchaser of the goods will seek to protect himself.

If there is a market in forward exchange, he can protect himself by its means. But then he will merely pass on the risk to the dealers in this market. And the risk will be all one way. Every one will want to buy future sterling and no one will want to sell it. The dealers must therefore be prepared to sell future sterling and not to buy. The dealers, in fact, will have to step in as *borrowers* of sterling and *lenders* of other currencies, to enable the traders to disregard variations in sterling. This amounts in substance to a disestablishment of sterling from its position as the money of account for international financing. Even if dealers could be found and the market created (sterling being supposed to be a fluctuating exception in a world of stable currencies), such an arrangement would be too artificial to last.[1]

---

[1] The purely speculative element in the market could be eliminated by the ingenious device recommended by Mr. Keynes for application to forward markets

The suggestion in the essay for the continuance of Government borrowing in America as an aid to the maintenance of the exchange had, as it turned out, little relevance to conditions as they were after the war. The investment market in America was extremely unfavourable to Government borrowing, at first owing to the trade activity and the omnivorous demands of trade for capital, then owing to the credit stringency which prevailed during the early part of the period of deflation (see IV, pp. 86-7).

But, however convenient, the raising of loans abroad was by no means essential to the maintenance of the value of sterling. If the pound steadily lost ground, till the collapse of February, 1920, momentarily brought the exchange down to 3·20, despite the simultaneous decline of the dollar itself in comparison with commodities, that was attributable above all to the absence of any adequate deterrent upon trade borrowing.

III.

No. III was read to the Economic Section of the British Association in September, 1919. Nearly a year had passed since the cessation of hostilities, and the time had apparently come to consider how the world could return to normal monetary conditions. The essay is entitled " The Gold Standard," and in it a return to the gold standard is assumed to be the only practicable solution of the problem.

The post-war inflation had just begun to make progress both in England and in the United States. That it was proceeding faster in the former was shown by the growing depreciation of sterling. The exchange, which remained not far from 4·70 for some time after the unpegging in March, 1919, had recently fallen rapidly, and was at about 4·20. The prohibition of the export of gold from America had ceased in June, 1919, and the heavy exports of gold which followed (to Spain, Japan, Argentina, and other parts of South America

in collapsed currencies (" Manchester Guardian," Supplement on Reconstruction, No. 1. Cf. also Res. 15 of the Financial Commission of the Genoa Conference, Cmd. 1667, p. 63).

and the East) helped to counteract the inflationary tendency
there. Since March, 1919, the export of gold from England
had been stopped, and that corrective was not operative here.
As inflation proceeded, the prospect of deflation became more
and more formidable. In September, however, the discount
on sterling was still below 15 per cent., and a devaluation of
sterling was not at that time an alternative to be seriously
thought of. The currencies of the European neutrals had
dropped one by one to a discount in relation to the dollar in the
first half of 1919, and Spain alone remained at or above par
till the end of the year. But for them too deflation was quite
a manageable policy.

On the other hand, the European belligerents were showing
graver symptoms. If inflation laid hold of England and
America and the European neutrals, that was because the
urgent demands of trade for fixed and circulating capital,
fostered and stimulated by cheap money, occasioned an unhealthy expansion of credit. The inflation from which the
European belligerents were suffering was an even graver disorder. They were still entangled in the financial troubles
which had originated in the war. Their Governments, unable
to raise genuine funds by tax or loan to cover their liabilities,
were resorting to the creation of bank credits and the printing
of paper money to meet the deficiency.

It had become clear that a devaluation of the currency
unit would be necessary for some of them. Austrian crowns
were at about 300 to £1, German marks at about 90. The
degree of depreciation was already such as to recall the precedent of the French Assignats, and to suggest that the crown,
if not the mark, might be discarded altogether, and cease to
be used as currency. Few people would have been found in
1919 to believe that a currency unit could suffer such a degree
of depreciation as have the mark and the crown in Austria,
Germany, Poland or Hungary during the last three years, and
yet continue to be regularly used as a medium of payment.
Even the rouble has preserved a continuous existence in
Soviet Russia, though there all pre-existing economic relations
based upon the monetary unit have themselves been swept
away by revolution.

But whatever measures might be necessitated by the collapse of currencies in Europe, it would be possible for the United States and Great Britain and other countries with healthy currencies to resume the gold standard as soon as their exchanges could be brought back to par.

The principal theme of No. III is the relation of the gold standard to the purchasing power or commodity value of gold, a matter on which more will remain to be said in the two concluding essays. The proposals put forward include a general adoption of a gold exchange standard. That is to say, currencies would ordinarily be made convertible *into one another*, through the foreign exchange market, convertibility into gold remaining in the background as an exceptional and infrequent alternative.

There is nothing very novel about such a scheme. It does not differ fundamentally from the practice which actually prevailed in Europe before the war, when many of the central banks used to hold a certain quantity of foreign balances, bills on foreign centres, or other liquid assets localised abroad. These foreign assets were freely drawn upon to avoid gold movements.

The same system has been resorted to in various forms in the British Empire. A fully developed exchange standard was in operation before the war in India, and the currencies of the Straits Settlements and several African possessions are at present tied to sterling by the same method. The credit arrangements of South Africa, Australia, and New Zealand are likewise based on London. These Dominions have not possessed an officially established exchange standard, but the most important of the banks have London offices and have in practice come to treat their sterling resources as their true reserves, exercising control over credit accordingly. During the wild fluctuations in the commodity value of sterling, which occurred in 1920 and 1921, the system failed to work smoothly. Sterling was first at a discount and then at a premium in South Africa. At one time the Australian banks found their sterling resources completely exhausted. But these were temporary aberrations, and the old system is now in operation again, though so long as sterling is at a discount, gold cannot play a part in it.

The general adoption of a gold exchange standard would therefore fully accord with the practical tendencies of banking at the present time. Such a standard forms part of the programme accepted at Genoa (see No. VI below).

IV.

No. IV was written in January, 1921, and its subject is the European currency situation at that time. But whereas No. III was concerned chiefly with the healthy currencies of Western Europe and America, No. IV deals more particularly with the collapsed currencies of Central and Eastern Europe. The opening of 1921 was a moment when there were good grounds for hopefulness. Hard upon the exchange panic of February, 1920, had followed a general recovery in the European currencies, and particularly of the collapsed currencies. If they appeared to lose ground again in the latter half of the year, that was because the commodity value of the dollars and pounds, by which they were measured in the exchange market, was being rapidly raised by severe deflationary measures. The German mark, in particular, though its value in relation to dollars and pounds was falling, was actually appreciating in real purchasing power, as measured by the prices of commodities. The effect on German public finances was notable. With a revival of confidence in the purchasing power of the mark, the Germans displayed a remarkable willingness to absorb Treasury bills, and the vast deficit of the year 1920-21 was successfully financed by their means. Liquid balances in the hands of the public had been reduced far below the convenient level in the course of the preceding flight from the mark, and it was the restoration of these balances during the subsequent reaction that produced this happy result. We have here an illustration of the effect first of active trade and then of depression upon cash balances and liquid resources.[1]

[1] Cf. V, pp. 119-20; see also " Currency and Credit," p. 110 and pp. 379-80.

The improvement was not confined to Germany. Partly as a result of the League of Nations Financial Conference held at Brussels in September, 1920, the paramount necessity of facing the budget situation was being more generally understood, and several of the distressed countries were making real efforts to increase their tax revenues. But the improvement was still very precarious. In the summer the mark gave way again, and for a time all the other currencies of Central and Eastern Europe seemed to be imperilled. In a few months, however, those countries (such as Czecho-Slovakia), which had made most progress towards recovery, emancipated themselves from the influence of the German currency. The state of utter demoralisation which has supervened in the present year has been confined to Germany, Austria, Poland, and Hungary.[1]

This renewed collapse has revived the question whether any or all of the currencies affected are likely to be abandoned altogether. Will there be a complete breach of monetary continuity? That can only happen if the paper money ceases to be used for the payment of *wages*. So long as it is so used, it will command a value equivalent to its wage-paying power. And it *must* be so used till a substitute is available.

For the first year or two after the armistice, when people were still unfamiliar with the behaviour of collapsed currencies, the internal value of the monetary units was much more stable than the external value. Prices and wages rose gradually under the influence of a growing note issue, but did not reflect the short-period fluctuations of the foreign exchange market. Gradually prices and wages have become more fluid, and in some instances, at any rate, prices are practically fixed in foreign currencies, and adjusted every morning and afternoon to the latest quotations of the exchange. Wages are also often adjusted at short intervals to an index number of the cost of living.

The discrepancies between internal and external prices, between one price and another and between prices and wages having thus been diminished, calculations of the future have

---

[1] Though some other countries, which have on this occasion successfully resisted the contagion, are by no means at the end of their difficulties.

become more possible, always provided that they are based on foreign currency units and that no cash balances or other assets fixed in the collapsed currency enter into the reckoning. Some of the difficulties in the way of a scheme of stabilisation have been sensibly diminished by the elimination of these price anomalies.

Nevertheless the position of the collapsed currency itself has become all the more precarious. The distrust of it has grown in proportion to the frequency and extent of the variations in its internal purchasing power. Austrian crowns, which are worth less than $\frac{1}{10000}$ as much as before the war, are indeed paid out week by week as wages, and spent in the shops. But no one will hold funds in crowns a day longer than is necessary.

Had a substitute been forthcoming, the crown would have vanished long ago. The French assignats fell out of use before they were demonetised by law, because a plentiful supply of gold and silver was at hand, partly hoarded in France, partly in circulation in neighbouring countries.

Very little gold or silver remains in private hands in Europe. Nevertheless considerable supplies of foreign paper money (dollars, pounds, Swiss francs, Czech crowns, etc.) are believed to be accumulated in the hands of the Austrians and Poles. These foreign currencies may quite possibly come to be used for wages, and retail payments. An employer, who is reluctant to keep a supply of depreciating Austrian crowns or Polish marks on hand, even for a week, may find it convenient one day to offer his workmen payment in foreign money. The workmen, if they believe that the shops will accept the money, will be willing to take it. If the practice spreads, the discredit of the native paper money will be suddenly hastened, and the transition will be accomplished.

Is this a danger to be feared, or is it a way of escape from a nightmare? It is both. To put an end to the use of discredited paper money, and to the lamentable confusion which has been introduced thereby into all economic relations, would bring the same sort of relief as was experienced in France on the return from the assignats to a metallic currency.

Nevertheless the change will be accompanied by a twofold danger. In the first place, though some employers possess a supply of foreign money, this will not be true of all. Those who have none will have the greatest difficulty in carrying on business. There will be the usual accompaniments of a scarcity of currency, acute depression, and widespread unemployment. Those with good credit will try to borrow, but the facilities for borrowing foreign currencies cannot be improvised in a moment. And those who cannot borrow will endeavour to sell. Goods will be thrown on the market. A new wave of distress will strain the social fabric.

Secondly, the financial difficulties of the Government will be suddenly brought to a head. The miserable pretence by which the expenses of administration are paid with fresh issues of paper money will be ended. State employees will go forth on pay-day with sheaves of new notes in their hands to beg a few centimes in the streets. Many examples are to be found, as in France under the Directorate or in Turkey to-day, when Governments, unable to raise adequate funds, have perforce let their liabilities fall into arrears. The peril is that, in the interval before the fiscal system can be adapted to the new monetary conditions, the power of the Government may be so completely paralysed as to reduce society to a state of anarchy.

If the monetary condition of some countries is thus desperate, the affairs of others which have been through acute currency troubles are approaching stability. The vexatious controls of prices and exchanges and restrictions on the movement of commodities, though perhaps less prevalent than they were, are still a serious evil. In particular, artificial control of the exchanges, though stigmatised by successive international conferences as " futile and mischievous," is continually being reimposed. To interfere with the freedom of any holder of paper currency, or of a bank credit payable in paper currency, to buy foreign currencies therewith is to discourage him from holding or acquiring funds so restricted. Such a policy can only aggravate the discredit of the paper money.

On the other hand, real progress has been made with the

abolition of food subsidies and food controls. The result has been both to relieve the national budgets and to remove an obstacle to production. And the relative inequalities among prices, wages, and exchanges have been diminished. In every way the return to normal conditions has thus been facilitated.

V.

No. V, on "The Federal Reserve System of the United States," was read to the Royal Statistical Society in February, 1922. A study of that system is essential to the problem of monetary reconstruction for two reasons.

First, the system is new, and has itself introduced a profound change into world monetary conditions. Before the war the greatest obstacle to any comprehensive reform of credit control (by which alone currency can be effectively dealt with) was the absence of a central banking system in the United States.[1] That defect has been remedied by the Federal Reserve Act of 1913.

Secondly, under present conditions, the value of gold means the value of the American dollar. The Federal Reserve Banks buy unlimited quantities of gold at the mint price of $20·67 per fine ounce. Fully 40 per cent. of the entire monetary stock of gold of the world is concentrated in the United States, and most of the remainder is shut away in the vaults of banks of issue or Treasuries in Europe and elsewhere, which have suspended specie payments. The commodity value of the dollar and therefore of gold is determined ultimately by the credit policy of the Federal Reserve banks. If we are to resume the use of gold as currency in the near future, our fate rests largely in their hands.

The essay deals partly with the machinery of the Federal Reserve system, partly with the manner in which that machinery has been used since it was set up.

In 1919 it was reasonable to fear that " if the countries which are striving to recover the gold standard compete with one another for the existing supply of gold, they will drive up

---

[1] See my " Good and Bad Trade," pp. 263-5.

the world value of gold, and will find themselves burdened with a much more severe task of deflation than they ever anticipated " (III, p. 56). The danger remains a reality (see VI, p. 135), but what has been happening in the past three years has been something very different. The world value of gold has been driven up, and to an extent that would hardly have been thought possible, had it not occurred. But it has not been driven up by any competition on the part of countries seeking to return to a gold standard. Unless those countries had adopted the very injudicious course of buying gold at a premium, their competition could not become effective till their currencies regained gold parity.

The rise in the commodity value of gold has been caused by a contraction of credit in the United States. During the latter part of 1920, as the dollar appreciated in terms of commodities, all the other currencies in the world became more and more depreciated relatively to it. In England and some other countries this relative depreciation was partly counter-acted by their own deflationary measures, and in 1921 they began to recover the lost ground. But they could not get back to par, and those countries, like Argentina and Japan, which had an effective gold standard in 1920, were compelled to abandon it. The United States thus became the only pur-chaser of gold as money, and remained so till the Swiss franc was restored to par in December, 1921.

Gold continued, of course, to be bought as a commodity, especially in the Far East. But subject to that demand, all the available supply—the raw production of the world's mines, the gold let loose from Soviet Russia, so much of their gold reserves as England and Holland have released—all has united in one broad stream to America to be bought with dollars by the Federal Reserve banks. The Federal Reserve banks have been able to outbid all competitors for the supply, because, though the *price* offered has remained fixed, the *value* of the dollars in which it is fixed has been steadily raised. They have been offering more and more real wealth in exchange for the gold.

In the last few months the tension has been relaxed. The

2

value of the dollar, both in commodities and in other currencies, has begun to fall again. The discount on sterling and other "healthy" currencies has diminished. This episode of the sudden enhancement of the commodity value of gold through a credit contraction in America remains, however, a significant example of that instability of the value of gold which was already apparent in 1919.

It is sometimes argued by the sceptics that neither the credit expansion of 1919-20 nor the subsequent contraction was affected or could have been affected by any action on the part of the Federal Reserve banks. But this argument would prove too much. The Federal Reserve banks ultimately put up the rediscount rate in order to save their cash reserves. That they can do so by this method is an assumption at the very foundation of the Federal Reserve Act. But how can they, unless their action will in some way or other affect the demands of the public for money? Of course the Federal Reserve Act *might* be based on a fallacy. But we have before us the fact that, when the Federal Reserve banks did take action, the anticipated effects followed, and with a startling thoroughness. It would be hard to point to any principle in the whole realm of political economy in the application of which experience has so amply confirmed theory and theory so successfully interpreted experience.

VI.

The final essay on "The Genoa Resolutions on Currency," is again concerned with the commodity value of gold. It may be indeed that the time for practical action towards monetary reconstruction has arrived. It is at any rate to be hoped that the stress of deflation and the bitterness of the trade depression are over. Clear signs of an inflationary reaction in America are appearing. Prices have risen in the present year, employment is improving, even wages are being raised in some industries. There have been grave labour disputes, but labour disputes have little or no ultimate effect on the progress of a

credit cycle.[1]   We have got back to something like the position
in which we stood in the summer of 1919.   Sterling is at a
discount of about 8 or 9 per cent.   Inflation is beginning as it
was beginning then to lower the commodity value of the dollar.
The great difference is that whereas in 1919 an inflationary
movement in this country, already impetuous enough, was
being stimulated by a regime of cheap money, now we are
still under the influence of the great deflation from which
America has just escaped.   Even here the prices of commodities have nearly ceased to fall, and it may be inferred with
some confidence that an early revival is in prospect.   But
whereas in 1919-20 the pound depreciated relatively to the
dollar, in the near future the dollar is likely to depreciate
relatively to the pound.

We may therefore expect the American Exchange soon to
be restored to par.[2]   Then will come the opportunity for a
settlement of the currency problem.   The Genoa resolutions
recognise the need for a stabilisation of gold itself.   Primarily
this is to guard against the value of gold being raised by "the
simultaneous and competitive efforts of countries to secure
metallic reserves," and, as mentioned above, this danger
remains a reality.   But the more *immediate* danger is just the
contrary.   America, having bought up all the surplus gold in
the world for two years, is encumbered with a gold reserve
so far beyond requirements that it has swamped the Federal
Reserve system.   To adapt the credit superstructure to this
reserve, on the basis of the Federal Reserve system as it
stands, would mean a portentous inflationary movement.   It
may perhaps be taken for granted that the Federal Reserve
Board will resist such a movement, but it is doubtful whether
they really have the power.   The purchase and deposit of
gold, in creating reserve deposits at the Federal Reserve
banks, has reduced the need for rediscounts within such narrow

---

[1] See " Good and Bad Trade," p. 146.

[2] An influence in the contrary direction is the newly increased American
Tariff.   How great its effect will be, and how far the effect will take the form of
hastening inflation in America rather than delaying the restoration of the exchange to par, it is impossible to predict.

limits that the New York rediscount rate has ceased to be effective. The rediscount rate stands at 4 per cent. (a low rate for American conditions), and the open market rate, instead of being 1 per cent. or so higher (V, p. 104, note) is, if anything, a fraction lower—3¾ to 4 per cent. With a revival of business there will come an increase in rapidity of circulation, and the existing stock of the means of payment (money and credit) will then be sufficient to support a higher level of commodity prices. If there is no increase in bank credits, there need be no increase in reserve deposits, or therefore in rediscounts, and the process may go far before the Federal Reserve banks are in a position to regain control.

We are therefore threatened with a renewed fall in the purchasing power of gold, which might be on as great a scale as that of 1919-20. We are now only too familiar with the troubles which accompany a period of inflation, and which more than outweigh the superficial advantages of a deceptive and fleeting prosperity. And "the greater the inflation, the more painful will be the process of deflation" (II, p. 42).

The only way to prevent the inflation is by keeping a tight hand on credit. This is the task of the Central banks. Suppose that the Federal Reserve banks in face of their redundant gold reserves and small rediscounts, are unable to exercise control. In a short time British and Dutch currencies, like those of Canada, Switzerland, and Sweden, will be at par. If and so far as the Central banks of these countries take steps to check any expansion of credit, they will begin to import gold from America, and this process will restore the Federal Reserve banks' control. Some degree of inflation is unavoidable, but by such means it can be kept within manageable limits, and if thereafter the purchasing power of gold and therefore of all the gold currency units is stabilised, there need be no deflation to follow.

It may perhaps be asked why, if dollars or pounds or both can be stabilised in terms of commodities, is it necessary to drag in gold at all? We used to build our currency systems upon gold as being itself a stabilising element. If the currencies can be themselves stabilised independently and gold is merely to derive its stability of value from them, what is the use of it?

The retention of gold is justifiable on other grounds than a mere concession to prejudice, or to the habits of financiers, whose scheme of things has been worked on the basis of a metal being available as a medium for the settlement of international balances of indebtedness. In an imperfect world, countries would be unwilling to leave the whole of their currency reserves in the form of credits or liquid assets held abroad. Not only might they be involved in war with a country where part of the reserve is held, but if the latter were involved in war with a third power, or exposed to some political cataclysm, its currency might suffer despite all international agreements, and the credits based upon it lose a part of their value. A gold exchange standard is a good practical plan, and is sufficiently free from this objection so long as the liquid resources held abroad are kept within the limits appropriate to working balances. But political stability must make much more progress before a purely paper standard stabilised by international control can be thought of.

Secondly, the proposal for stabilisation cannot pretend to have passed beyond the experimental stage. It is easy to argue that it is practicable and desirable. But practical men can hardly be asked to contemplate the demonetisation of gold, till experience has proved that it can be dispensed with.

Thirdly, the interests of the gold market itself cannot be ignored. The production of gold is an important industry. From time immemorial the market has been dominated by the monetary demand, and in recent years, both before and since the war, a great part of the annual production of the mines has gone to meet that demand. Were that demand withdrawn, the industrial demand would be insufficient to absorb the annual supply, and a fall of price and consequent loss to the producers would ensue. This loss the producers might be expected to put up with, if it were the end of the matter. But their interests would be more profoundly threatened by the release of the accumulated stocks of gold. These stocks are so vast (VI, p. 136) that to let them loose would utterly disorganise the gold market, and the consequent collapse in the value of gold would inflict heavy loss on all the possessors of gold reserves. The loss would equally fall on all creditors whose rights are expressed in gold, and it is scarcely necessary to point out that the present is a time when debts expressed in gold possess a quite exceptional importance in the realm of international finance.

For all these reasons it would be a serious error to entangle any project of monetary reconstruction with a demonetisation of gold. Nevertheless that does not mean that we must resume the gold standard as soon as the pound sterling gets back to par, whether the difficulties in regard to the future purchasing power of gold have been provided against or not. It is not easy to promote international action, and should it fail, the wisest course for the time being might be to concentrate on the stabilisation of sterling in terms of commodities, rather than to tie the pound to a metal, the vagaries of which cannot be foreseen. An interesting precedent is to be found in the action during the war, of the Scandinavian countries and Spain, in suspending the free coinage of gold and the purchase of gold at mint price by their Central banks. This they did to save their currencies from depreciating along with gold, and in fact their paper money rose at one time to a very substantial premium in terms of gold.

But whatever emergency measure might be desirable, to avoid the contagion of a renewed inflationary movement in the gold standard countries, it may be taken for granted that any permanent settlement of the world's currencies must be based upon gold.

I.

THE FALL IN THE AMERICAN EXCHANGE.[1]

IT is commonly said that the recent fall in the New York Exchange on London is due to the enormous increase in imports from the United States into this country and the substantial decrease in our exports sent in return. In seeking remedies the problem is stated to be that of " paying for our imports." In a sense of course this is true, but it is only partially true, and unless carefully qualified is apt to be very misleading.

The fact is that this phenomenon of adverse foreign exchanges is common to all the belligerent nations, and in the case of France, Germany, Russia, Austria-Hungary, and Italy it is well recognised to be due to the currency inflation caused by excessive issues of inconvertible paper money. In England we have successfully maintained the convertibility of our paper money, and it circulates side by side with gold and at its par value. But we have not escaped inflation, and the fall in the American Exchange is merely a symptom of that inflation. In time of peace gold can pass readily from one country to the other, and the inflation would have corrected itself at an earlier stage by relatively moderate exports of gold. When the export of gold is obstructed, a gold currency behaves very much as an inconvertible paper currency would, and it is thus possible for a gold currency, or a paper currency effectively and genuinely convertible into gold, to become inflated.

The inflation has been caused by an excessive creation of credit money. Loans from the banks to the Government were practically added to the assets side of the bankers' balance sheets, with the result of course that an equal addition was made

[1] Written in September, 1915.

23

on the liabilities side.   An addition to the liabilities of the banks means an addition to the nation's stock of credit money.   If people's balances on current account had been sufficient before the war, they became more than sufficient, and, as it is wasteful to keep money on current account earning no interest, the additional money tended to be spent or invested.   But however much it is spent or invested this credit money merely passes from one person to another, and continues to exist, *so long as the banks do not reduce the aggregate amount of their loans.* Thus the amount of money spent every day was greater than before, and the demand for commodities and for labour was correspondingly greater.   Prices rose, or, in other words, as a result of the increase in the supply of money, the value of money in commodities diminished.

This is what is meant by inflation, and the effect on the foreign exchanges is easy to see.   If in this country money is being spent more rapidly and prices are higher than in normal times, a more favourable market is offered for foreign commodities, and at the same time part of the surplus which might otherwise be exported is taken up by the domestic demand. Thus the excessive creation of credit money of itself tends to produce an adverse balance of trade.   In time of peace the balance would be paid for by an export of gold, and the loss of gold would lead immediately to a curtailment of credit through the instrumentality of a high rate of interest, and thus equilibrium would be restored.   When the export of gold is impossible, and no steps are taken to curtail credits, the demand for remittances turns the foreign exchanges against us, and this tendency will work until the loss on exchange is sufficient to offset the high prices caused by the inflation, and the English market ceases to be abnormally profitable to the foreign merchant.   It should be observed, however, that this disturbance of equilibrium and its correction do not in practice extend over any appreciable period.   Probably there is no noticeable disturbance of equilibrium at all.   The movement of the exchanges proceeds *pari passu* with the inflation, and *prevents* the occurrence of any considerable uncovered balance of imports.

To the foregoing theory it may be objected that as a matter of fact the inflation has been going on ever since the beginning of the war, while the American Exchange has only quite recently turned at all seriously against us. The explanation of this is as follows. Before the war, England was a lending nation. Although our imports always exceeded our exports, nevertheless a part of our exports always represented new foreign investments, and the excess of imports would have been much greater but for those investments. When war broke out, we at once ceased to lend to foreign nations and began, to a greater or less extent, to borrow from them, chiefly by selling them securities. Trade had to accommodate itself to a greatly increased excess of imports. Now the supply of currency and credit money in England and the United States respectively, and the relative price levels in the two countries were adjusted to the pre-war conditions. In order that imports from the United States to England might be increased, the market for American commodities in England had to be improved, and, until that happened, the American who had to remit money to London found an insufficiency of remittances in the contrary direction. The exchange therefore turned violently against America. At that time it was possible for England to indulge in a very considerable degree of inflation before the exchange even reached the equilibrium point. The additional credit money created and put into circulation was for several months no more than sufficient to create a market for the additional imports which, by reason of the intrinsic strength of our financial position, we were in a position to pay for. For example, it might be that when the aggregate amount of credit money in the United Kingdom was 1000 millions, the annual excess of imports was 150 millions, and that an additional 150 millions of credit money was no more than sufficient to make English markets so favourable as to attract an additional 200 millions of imports. By stopping our foreign investment, and to some extent selling securities, we were probably in a position to pay for an additional 200 millions of imports a year from the very beginning of the war, and therefore, on the assumption adopted, we could create 150 millions of additional credit money without turning the exchanges against us. By the time this amount of credit money had been created, the neutral exchanges would be at par, and there would be a steady annual excess of imports of 350 millions instead of the 150 millions of peace time. But if *more* than 150 millions of credit money was created and began to circulate, then, if the exchanges remained at par, a greater excess of imports than 350 millions would be created. If this further excess of imports could not be paid for by the sale of securities or by direct borrowings from neutral countries, and if it was impracticable to pay for it in gold, it could not be paid for at all, and the effort to pay for it would at once turn the exchanges against us. The fall in the value of sterling in terms of neutral currencies would make the English market proportionally less attractive to neutral merchants, and would tend to counteract the artificial demand for commodities arising from the excessive amount of credit money in circulation. The extent of the fall would tend to be just sufficient to keep down the excess of imports to the amount we could pay for. The foregoing explanation may be applied *mutatis mutandis* to all the belligerents, and helps us to see why the exchanges turned against Russia and Austria at the very beginning of the war, against Germany after about two months, against France after about nine months, and against ourselves after nearly a year. We are the greatest lending nation, France comes next, and then Germany, while Austria and Russia are not lending nations at all.

It appears then that the problem is not how to pay for our imports. Great as is the excess of imports, it is probable that there is no uncovered balance to pay for. The fall in the exchange must be remedied, if at all, by reducing the excessive supply of credit money in this country, or by increasing the supply of credit money in the United States.

The transfer of gold does but little in this direction. Our paper currency has very little relation at present to our gold reserves, while the American banks are reluctant to create new credits to the full extent which their growing stocks of gold would permit.

The measure most commonly proposed, of large borrowings by our Government in New York, is usually advocated as enabling us to pay for our imports. If, as is argued above, we are not importing more than we can pay for, this reasoning is not valid. It is true nevertheless that large loans in New York might do much to ease the situation. The swollen credits on this side are a by-product of the immense borrowings in London, and if borrowings in New York could to some extent be substituted for borrowings in London in future, the tendency to inflation would be diminished here, and a similar tendency might be produced to a greater or less extent in America. But it is not safe to expect very much from this. Large borrowing operations only lead to the creation of new credit money when they overstrain the market upon which they are carried out. It is probable that the American bankers will refuse to let their market be overstrained. They have had bitter experience in the past of the crises brought about by inflation and the painful process of " deflation," and they are reluctant to take any course now which might start that disastrous train of events again. If any loans in America are confined to the amounts that can be taken by *bona fide* investors, the effect in relieving the London market and so moderating inflation here will be comparatively small.

There remains one other method of diminishing credits here, that is to say, a high rate of discount or of interest on temporary loans. This is in normal times the recognised remedy for inflation, and for the adverse foreign exchanges and exports of gold which accompany inflation. Indeed the only arguments against this method are that the times are not normal, and that either it will not produce the same effects as in peace time, or it will have other evil effects which will make it on the whole undesirable.

It is argued that a high rate of interest will not have the same effects as in peace time, because the greater part of the production of the country is being carried on for the Government, and, as it *must* continue, it cannot be discouraged or restricted in any degree by high rates for borrowed money. This argument is not wholly without force, but at the most it only proves that production will not be so sensitive to a high rate of interest as under normal conditions. In point of fact it is probable that less than half the production of the country is being carried on for the Government, and the remainder would be as sensitive as ever. And even the portion which is dealing with Government orders could, under pressure, diminish the amount of accommodation which it asks from the banks.

The loans and advances of the banks are ordinarily made, for the most part, to manufacturers and dealers to meet the cost of goods in course of manufacture or in transit or awaiting sale. To the manufacturer, no doubt, the interest he pays on money borrowed during the period of manufacture is quite a small item in the cost of production, and hardly affects the price which he quotes when offered an order. It is the dealer or merchant whose business is sensitive to the rate of interest, especially the wholesale dealer, whose profit is a small percentage on his turn-over, and may be completely eaten up by an extra 2 or 3 per cent. per annum on the money he borrows. The effect of a high rate of interest is to discourage dealers from holding stocks of commodities; and they diminish their stocks partly by lowering prices to the consumer, but chiefly by giving fewer orders to the manufacturers and importers. Borrowings are thus diminished by means of a diminution of the stocks of commodities in the country awaiting sale.

At the present time the Government is spending some £1,200,000,000 a year, while the total expenditure of the community, which immediately before the war must have been fully £2,400,000,000, must now, with the inflated prices which prevail, be nearly £3,000,000,000. So far as the Government expenditure is concerned the merchant is almost completely eliminated, and the banks are therefore relieved of his demands. Consequently the money advanced by the banks directly or indirectly to the Government is to some extent *in substitution for* the advances which would otherwise have been needed to finance the commodities produced by that portion of our productive resources which is now supplying the Government.

The balance of the banks' advances is mainly required for

financing the remainder of our present production, which on the figures given above would amount to some £1,800,000,000. This portion of the advances would be as sensitive to a high bank rate as in time of peace. Just as in time of peace, the merchants would find it expensive to hold large stocks, and would curtail their orders to manufacturers both here and abroad.

Now this curtailment of orders, which in normal times causes unemployment and distress to the working classes and loss to the manufacturers, is just what is wanted at the present time. We are suffering from a scarcity of labour which interferes both with recruiting and with the supply of munitions. We are suffering from adverse foreign exchanges, which would be partially rectified if fewer orders were given abroad for commodities not needed by the Government or for Government work. We are suffering from an inflation of credit which increases money prices against both the Government and the private consumer, and which is the primary cause of the adverse exchanges, and this inflation could be reduced by a measure which will cut down the bankers' balance sheets on both sides.

Moreover, the people who at the beginning of the war were prophesying widespread unemployment during the war are now prophesying widespread unemployment on the restoration of peace, and with much better reason. After 1815 a period of acute distress set in, which was probably due almost entirely to the painful process of deflating a currency inflated under the strain of war finance. The distress after the war will be acute in proportion as the inflation is allowed to get out of hand.

Against these advantages, however, certain objections can be urged which are sufficiently serious or at any rate plausible to require answering.

First of all it must be admitted that a drastic and effective raising of the bank rate always causes something of a shock to business. An inflation of credit is accompanied by expanding markets and rising prices, and, if the inflation is suddenly arrested and reversed, the consequent contraction of demand

and fall of prices will disappoint the expectations of borrowers and lenders alike, and may cause many failures. This has to be faced in time of peace, but perhaps it may be desirable at any cost to postpone such a catastrophe in time of war. As a matter of fact, however, there is no reason why a high bank rate should cause anything in the nature of a crisis. The peculiar convulsive character of a financial crisis, such as those periodically experienced in the last hundred years, is due to the sudden shortage of legal tender money, which threatens perfectly solvent banks with failure, so that they are compelled to restrict credits at all costs. But we are now provided with an almost indefinitely expansible emergency currency, and high rates could be left to work out their consequences gradually, without any of that ruthless refusal of credit which is the usual cause of the failures in a crisis. Even very high rates only inflict quite moderate losses *directly* on the borrowers. More serious losses follow as soon as the restriction of advances and consequent diminution of the stock of credit money makes itself felt in a diminished demand for commodities, but the failures occasioned by these losses only mature gradually, and could hardly be extensive enough to produce anything in the nature of a crisis.

Another possible objection is that, if the rate of interest were raised, it would be raised against the State, who is now the principal borrower. In point of fact, however, the high rates which are necessary to correct an inflation of credit never have to last long, and when they have begun to take effect they can safely be lowered even below the rates which previously prevailed. The rate of interest which borrowers are willing to pay depends on the rate of profit they expect to make by using the money borrowed. In times of inflation, when demand is increasing and prices are rising, stocks of commodities grow in value while they lie in the shop or warehouse; business is thus exceptionally profitable, and borrowers can readily pay a rate of interest which at other times would be regarded as high. But if they are made to pay a rate which is a little higher still, and borrowing is checked, the amount of credit money begins to diminish, demand falls off, prices fall, and the holding of stocks of commodities results in a loss, which has to be added to the rate of interest and may make even an apparently low rate burdensome. It almost invariably happens that after a financial crisis there is a period of very low interest. If we permit the present inflation to continue, prices will go on rising, and a high rate of interest will come of itself simply through business becoming abnormally profitable, and whereas perhaps it might now be possible to check the inflation with a 7 per cent. bank rate, it may be that in a few months 10 per cent. will hardly be high enough. In fact, whereas money was being lent at 2 to 2½ per cent. a few months ago when the inflation was being started, 4½ or 4 per cent. now counts as a low rate. The inflation itself puts up the rate of interest against the Government, and a relatively short period of high rates would soon enable us to borrow on more favourable terms than before.

A third possible objection is that if we restrict the supply of credit money the subscriptions to War Loans will fall off, simply because there will not be a sufficient supply of credit money to take them up. But when an abnormal activity of business has been produced by an inflation of credits, manufacturers and traders need greater bank balances in hand, and can spare no more for investment than in ordinary conditions, while when the banks have been creating credits on a large scale to finance this business activity they are not in a position to create further credits to take up war loans. It is a common experience that when trade is active there is a scarcity of capital, and new issues on apparently liberal and attractive terms are left in large quantities on the underwriters' hands. This was conspicuously so in 1912 and 1913.

A fourth possible objection is that the inflation which it is sought to correct cannot be diminished by a high bank rate because it is due to the increased issues of paper currency. But so long as currency notes are issued practically on demand to any one who has a credit at the Bank of England, the way to diminish the circulation is by diminishing credits. In fact, the demand for legal tender currency is determined by the supply of credit money, and when a crisis is precipitated through a shortage of legal tender money, the remedy is always found in a restriction of credits.

Of course the remedy of a high bank rate is a far-reaching one, and has other consequences, as shown above, which are quite equal in importance to its effects on the foreign exchanges. Its justification is that the adverse exchanges are merely a symptom of the evil of inflation, to which a number of other detrimental effects are equally traceable, such as scarcity of labour, high prices, and even high rates of interest.

Inflation itself may be regarded as a symptom of financial weakness. When Governments find it necessary to borrow on a vast scale they may outrun the supply of savings available for investment. They then have to resort to the bankers, who can lend money by merely creating credits. It is the creation of these credits which makes the pound sterling unduly plentiful and therefore cheap in terms of commodities and of neutral currencies. But by allowing the rate of interest to remain low, we are encouraging merchants to ask for credits and to order goods from both domestic and foreign producers. We are thus artificially increasing our difficulties, and weakening our financial position at the very time when it is being subjected to the greatest possible strain.

II.

INFLATION.[1]

INFLATION is not very easy to define, but in reference to the actual circumstances of the present time, perhaps, it is not very important to arrive at an accurate definition. It matters more to investigate what has happened to the circulating medium of this and other countries, and what tendencies are at work, than to decide whether any particular conditions ought or ought not to be called inflation.

In all the principal belligerent countries other than Great Britain legal tender paper currencies, which before the war were convertible into gold, have been made inconvertible; a part of the cost of the war has been met by advances in notes from the note-issuing banks to the Governments; the note issues have been thereby increased to excess, and the value of the currency units has been depreciated below the former gold par. This process is the almost universal symptom of an overstrain of Government finance. A Government which *must* raise £100,000,000 issues a loan and obtains genuine subscriptions to the amount of only £50,000,000; the deficiency is made up by the creation of paper money; in the last resort there may be no other course open.

In this country conditions are rather different. Deposit banking is so highly developed here that if the necessary sums cannot be raised by borrowing from the public, the deficiency is made up not by the issue of paper money, but in the first instance by the creation of banking credits.

The addition of, say, £50,000,000 to the assets of the banks necessarily involves the addition of £50,000,000 to their

[1] Written in September, 1916.

liabilities, and in particular to their demand liabilities ; and the demand liabilities of a banker are, from the point of view of the depositors, money.   By this creative act the bankers increase the supply of money for the purposes of business by so much ; for credits are the only form of money required for transactions between one business man and another.   With credit money, as with paper money, an increase of supply produces a depreciation of value.   The sudden accession of purchasing power in the business world, over and above what was necessary for the extent and character of its operations before, stimulates purchases beyond the amount that can be supplied from existing stocks and sources of production.   Dealers and manufacturers can only check this stimulation of purchases by a general rise of prices, which will in turn lead to a general rise of wages.   In ordinary times, when we have a gold currency in general use, and a strict limit on the issues of paper, any such wholesale extension of credits as is here in question would be impossible.   When even a much more moderate extension occurs, the consequent rise in money values produces after an interval a demand for more legal tender currency.   Gold is withdrawn for internal use, passes into circulation through the payment of wages, and under the influence of high working-class earnings remains in circulation. These withdrawals of gold, which come of course from the Bank of England's reserve, cannot be replaced from abroad. The rise in money values here will have stimulated purchases from abroad and diminished exports, and, far from gold coming in from abroad, it will tend rather to go out.   The Bank of England in such a case protects its reserve by an increase in the bank rate and the consequent general restriction of credits.

In the present war this restrictive tendency has at one point ceased to work.   The Government are prepared to issue whatever amount of currency notes may be needed for internal circulation.   The drain of gold abroad remains.   But so large a part of the civilised world has had recourse to inconvertible paper currencies under the stress of war, that, apart from this country, the gold-using portion of the world is restricted to the United States and half a dozen relatively small neutral countries in Europe and America. The gold displaced from circulation by the currency notes or drawn from reserve here, together with the new production of gold in the British Empire, is so considerable in proportion to the pre-existing stocks of gold in these countries that there has up to now been an expansion in their currency and credit systems almost, if not quite, in proportion to that which has taken place in Great Britain. Consequently even after exporting enough gold to maintain the principal foreign exchanges at a fairly respectable level, we still have a large stock in reserve. In one sense, since we have preserved the convertibility and gold value of our currency, we have avoided inflation. But this is only because we have succeeded in inducing a very considerable inflation of gold itself, so that the value of gold in commodities in the United States, for example, has depreciated approximately as much as the value of our currency notes.

It seems likely that as long as the war lasts this situation will continue. Government borrowings, whether by way of large long-term loans, or by way of the continuous issue of short-term securities, will produce a continually growing inflation. Even in so far as the short-term securities are taken not by the banks but by merchants or manufacturers, those securities tend to be treated by the holders as the equivalent of cash, so that they add to the inflation almost as much as if they had been used by the banks as the basis of fresh credits. As the inflation grows, the exchanges on London will be maintained by a steady stream of gold to the United States and other gold-using neutrals. Of course ultimately our power of sending gold may be exhausted, but until that happens we certainly escape a part of the disadvantages of inflation ordinarily so called. The high prices, the artificially stimulated trade, the relatively low real wages, the high rate of interest, these accompaniments of inflation we experience, but we avoid the suspension of specie payments, the disparity of our currency with foreign currencies, and the sacrifice of our position as the clearing-house of the world's trade.

But if our supply of gold lasts to the end of the war, what

will be our situation on the restoration of peace? This question raises a problem which is complex enough in itself, and which is made all the more difficult by the impossibility of foreseeing what new developments may yet take place. There are nevertheless some broad tendencies, which can be distinguished, and which may clearly be expected to form important elements in the solution.

During the war there is a shortage of capital for purposes other than war-like supplies. From the point of view of investment this shortage of capital is manifested in two directions. On the one hand there is little long-term investment in new issues; on the other the temporary advances made by bankers for the purposes of business are curtailed. From the point of view of industry and commerce these tendencies make themselves felt, the former in a failure to extend, to renew or even to maintain the plant, buildings, railways, ships, etc., which constitute the permanent capital of the country; the latter in a diminution of stocks of goods (other than war-like supplies) in course of manufacture or transit or awaiting sale.

On the restoration of peace there will be a great pressure on the part of merchants, manufacturers, and others, to remedy these deficiencies, and to borrow money for the purpose if necessary.

Now it must be observed that the mere need of the manufacturers and merchants to have money for capital renewals will not of itself create that money. Their demand for capital renewals will only be effective in so far as they either possess or can borrow the necessary funds. Up to the end of the war the Government will practically monopolise the market for capital. On the restoration of peace there will be an abrupt or at any rate a very rapid change. During the war the population of the country, especially the richer portion, restricts expenditure on consumable commodities in order to provide money for the Government by way either of loans or of taxes. Of the £1,300,000,000 or thereabouts, which the Government is borrowing in a year, a considerable portion is no doubt borrowed from abroad; a considerable portion again is furnished by the creation of banking credits; but the balance, which is probably much more than half the total, is made up of the genuine savings of the public. For a short time after the end of the war the Government will have to go on borrowing, but very soon to a diminishing extent. As soon as it stops altogether, the whole of the hundreds of millions per annum which the savings of the public have produced for the war will become available for other purposes, and largely (though not entirely) for industrial and commercial investment. It might be argued perhaps that the cessation of war expenditure would produce a great contraction of the annual turn-over of money. But this cannot be so, to any considerable extent. The war expenditure, so long as it continues, is perpetually replenishing the banking accounts of the capitalists, and the pockets of the workmen who are engaged in the production of war-like supplies. When the war expenditure is finally wound up, one last distribution of money will be made among these recipients. They, however, will not want to hold the money idle. They will spend it just as rapidly as during the war, and they will spend it either (1) on consumable commodities, or (2) on investments. If there is no tendency to hold back larger sums from these purposes than there was during the war, there will be as great a turn-over of money per unit of time as before. During the war the turn-over of money has been swollen in proportion to the expansion of credits; after the peace it will be similarly swollen. The expenditure of this swollen money income, in so far as it is applied to consumable commodities, will draw upon the already depleted stocks, and merchants will be compelled to defend their stocks by raising prices, and to replenish them by giving orders to the manufacturers. The consequent activity of trade will lead to a demand from the manufacturers, (a) for more fixed capital, and (b) for temporary accommodation to finance production.

As regards the demand for fixed capital this must be met mainly from the funds derivable from the investor, British or foreign, though to some extent money can be provided directly or indirectly for the purpose by way of temporary advances, e.g. advances to the Stock Exchange which are used indirectly to finance new issues, or advances to manufacturers of machinery, etc., in anticipation of payment on the completion of contracts.

From the point of view of an examination of the causes and effects of inflation, the crucial question is that of the provision of temporary advances, which are mainly needed to finance dealers who are carrying stocks of goods, or manufacturers who are producing them. It is these temporary advances which ordinarily form the greater part of the assets of bankers. Under war conditions not only have the bankers' assets been swollen by the addition of large blocks of Government securities, both long and short dated, but these securities have encroached on the domain of advances to traders. The shrinkage in advances corresponds to the shrinkage of stocks which has been already referred to. In some degree the shrinkage of stocks may be less than the shrinkage of advances. Under the influence of caution and of high rates of interest, dealers should tend in war time to apply surplus profits in reduction of borrowing. This means practically the investment of their savings in a reduction of temporary borrowing, but it is probably confined within moderate limits owing to the strong inducements held out to put the savings in Government securities. There is another direction also in which there is a shrinkage of advances which does not correspond to any shrinkage in stocks of goods, for during the war new issues of capital are restricted, and the facilities for Stock Exchange speculation are reduced. But even when allowance is made for these exceptions, it remains true that a very large part of the reduction in the banks' advances to traders represents a reduction in stocks of goods, a reduction attributable not only to the restriction of credit, but to the diversion of labour and plant to war purposes, and to the diminished turn-over of nearly all commodities other than warlike supplies.

On the restoration of peace and the revival of demand for these commodities, there will be, as stated above, a demand for loans for the replenishment of stocks. If the bankers meet

this demand it will mean an increase in their assets and consequently also in their liabilities ; in other words, there will be a
renewed increase in credits and a renewed tendency to inflation,
unless, that is, some counteracting influence is introduced. In
ordinary times this counteracting influence would be found in
the loss of gold, partly for internal circulation, partly for export.
To check this double drain of gold the bank rate would be
raised; the situation would then be restored by the effect of
the high bank rate in discouraging borrowers and so diminishing credits. Under war conditions the internal drain of
gold is prevented by the issue of currency notes. The unre-
stricted issue of currency notes may or may not continue after
the restoration of peace, but in any case the drain of gold for
export will be a danger signal. Quite apart from any further
inflation of credits the export of gold is likely to be a serious
matter as soon as the gold is free to move, without excessive
charges for insurance, etc., to places where the exchange is
anything from 2 to 7 per cent. against us. We might lose
practically the whole of our remaining reserve of gold even if
there were no increase of the inflation, and it seems likely
therefore that it will be urgently necessary to take steps, if not
to reduce the existing inflation, at any rate to prevent it from
increasing. Tradition and practice would be in favour of
accomplishing this by a sufficient increase of the bank rate.
This measure is always unpopular with a large section of
opinion in the City; but the chief ground of its unpopularity
is that it accomplishes its purpose; for a restriction of credits
depresses business, while inflation stimulates it and makes it
profitable. An alternative is to restrict advances directly by
means of an arrangement come to among the bankers. This
at the time when measures of reconstruction are to be initiated
is also likely to be unpopular. There remains another method.
The bankers' balance sheets are swollen by the inclusion of
Government securities. If any considerable part of these
securities could be redeemed by money raised not from the
banks but from the public, the balance sheets would be
correspondingly reduced. Whatever sum was so applied
could be lent out again by the banks without creating any

greater inflation than existed before. But if the money is
borrowed from the public, it will be subtracted from the funds
available for the restoration of our fixed capital. And perhaps
the only way in which this remedy could be applied, consistently with the needs of reconstruction, is by raising the
money by taxation. It is to be feared that the prolongation
of the full burden of war taxation for the first year or two of
the peace would be at least as unpopular as either of the other
remedies.

But if the possible remedies for inflation all have this
apparently oppressive character, would it not be best, perhaps,
after all to let the inflation run its course? This is not an
alternative to be scouted as out of the question. It is at any
rate necessary to compare its disadvantages with those attend-
ant on the other course. That the continuance of inflation
means the continuance and indeed enhancement of war prices
after the conclusion of peace is in itself only a minor disadvantage. The difference is only one of degree, since in any
case a great part of the war-time inflation and therefore of war
prices is bound to continue. The consumer would grumble;
but inflation means not only high prices but high wages, and
(in so far as the growth of wages falls short of the growth of
prices) good employment. The recipient of fixed interest or
dividends would suffer, but on the other hand profits and
variable dividends would be increased. There would be some
hardship and injustice, but hardly so great as to be a conclusive
argument against continued inflation.

The crux of the matter is to be found in the foreign
exchange position. Before the war international debts were
settled in London. The position of London as the world's
clearing-house has always been profitable, but its importance
is not to be measured by the direct profit. Its real importance
lies in the financial strength which it gives us. To support the
international financial transactions which take place, there
must always be large balances in London. These transactions
include not merely the financing of a vast volume of international trade, but also great investment transactions, which
require balances proportionate to the large payments involved.

At any moment, therefore, there are large foreign balances in London, which give English financial houses a far greater command of funds for capital purposes than they could otherwise have, while the central position of London in the foreign exchange market enables them to direct these funds whither they will without difficulty.   In connection with post-war commercial policy much stress is laid on the importance of diminishing the financial and commercial control which the Germans have aimed at exercising, and to some extent have really exercised, all over the world.   This control is trifling compared to the control which this country has exercised, and while the Germans have had to travel to the ends of the earth to find their opportunities, we have gained ours by sitting still in the City and letting the whole financial world come to us. Many causes have contributed jointly to bring about this result. Our start of some half a century or more over the rest of the world in developing modern industry; our geographical position; our special aptitude for shipping; our possession of so large a part of the resources of the world in the British Empire; these and many other influences, both transitory and permanent, have helped.   But it is a *necessary* condition of our tenure of the position of the world's clearing-house that we must have a trustworthy currency.   It is now nearly a century since the Bank of England resumed specie payments after the Napoleonic Wars.   Since then we have consistently maintained a free gold standard.   Latterly we have held the position of the only really free gold market among a world of nations nearly all of whom had adopted gold as the legal measure of value.   This has contributed enormously to confirm our position.   It is quite conceivable that in the future the world may adopt some other standard than gold, for gold is itself subject to great and even violent fluctuations of value. Such a change would raise difficult questions as to the provision of a stable and trustworthy unit of value in London; but till it occurs it is of supreme importance that we should not sacrifice our commanding position by failing to maintain the value of sterling in gold.   Suppose that we do so fail; that practically all our stock of gold is demanded for export;

that we suspend specie payments; that sterling falls to a
discount as compared both with gold and with foreign
currencies. No one can set a limit to the fall in the value of
sterling once it begins. Any commercial transaction financed
in London may turn out a fiasco. If Chili floats a loan in
London, the value of the proceeds may fall by 10 per cent. in
the interval between its first announcement and the receipt
of the proceeds. The profit on a cargo sent from Buenos
Ayres to Europe may be turned into a loss before it arrives.
Once really serious distrust of our unit of value sets in, foreign
firms will no longer be willing to draw on London, there will
no longer be any reason for maintaining balances in London,
and there will be a rush to withdraw the balances entrusted
there. These balances are, of course, really demand liabilities
of London banks, and their wholesale withdrawal would add
to the natural depreciation of sterling, arising from the inflation
of credits, a panic depreciation to which it would be difficult to
set a limit.

Of course such a calamity would only occur if the future
maintenance of the value of sterling were really distrusted.
Specie payments might actually be suspended for a time
without causing any such distrust. But that would only be
possible if it were quite clear that the Government and the
Bank of England were both able and willing to apply adequate
remedies. Thus *sooner or later* these remedies must be
adopted, and there is every advantage in adopting them
sooner rather than later. The greater the inflation, the more
painful will be the process of deflation. The more dependent
manufacturers and merchants have become on inflated prices,
the more likely they are to fail when the prices are reduced.
During the period of inflation, money wages rise. When
credits are curtailed, and prices fall, it is no longer possible to
give employment at these high wages; unemployment and
labour disputes follow; and the extent of these evils will be
proportionate to the extent of the curtailment of credits
and the fall of prices. The high profits which are the result
of rising prices during a period of inflation enable borrowers
to pay a high rate of interest. The greater the inflation the

higher must be the deterrent rate of interest required to check it.

If, when peace brings its pressure for new credits and its renewed freedom in the movement of gold, the situation is allowed to drift, this will mean that the unpleasant remedies are not avoided, but only postponed, and their postponement will make them more unpleasant. But besides the three measures suggested above, an increase of the bank rate, a restriction of credit facilities, and a redemption of a portion of the Government securities held by the banks, there is another measure which at first sight promises relief by smoother means than any of these. In the special circumstances of this country the really serious consequences of excessive inflation arise from the depreciation of sterling in the foreign exchanges. If the Government intervenes to regulate the exchanges and succeeds in maintaining them at par, or near enough to par to check the export of gold, these consequences will be avoided. The method of so regulating the exchanges is to borrow in foreign countries and to sell the credits thus obtained to any one who wishes to remit. When the exchanges are merely deranged by a temporary disturbance of the balance between exports and imports this method is completely effective; in essence a sum equal to the temporary discrepancy between exports and imports is borrowed (or repaid) and the balance of trade is so maintained. But here we are concerned with a derangement of the exchanges arising from a more deep-seated cause; credit money has become unduly plentiful and unduly cheap in terms of foreign currencies. Unless this disturbing cause is removed, the remedy must continue to be applied for an indefinitely long time. If, for example, this method is applied to the exchange between London and New York, traders here who wish to import American goods will hand over money to the Government in exchange for dollars in New York. If the Government applies the money received in London to reducing the amount of credit money in London (e.g. by buying Government securities from the banks), it will be reducing the excess of credit money here and will soon restore the exchange to equilibrium. If it spends the money, e.g. applies it to buying American securities, to redeeming debt in the hands of the public, or to making advances to assist traders, the inflation remains untouched, and the Government will have to go on raising loan after loan in America without doing any permanent good.

The redemption of Government securities in the hands of the banks is really only the last of the three possible remedies enumerated above, presented in a slightly different form, the necessary funds being raised abroad instead of at home. But even this method may be applied in vain. Bankers are accustomed to regulate the credits they grant by the amount of money they hold in reserve or at call. If the amount of legal tender money in the country is limited, then a tendency to grant excessive credits is checked as soon as the consequent demand for more money for circulation begins to deplete the bankers' reserves. But when, as at present, the amount of legal tender money that can be obtained by the banks is practically unlimited, this check does not work. When the Government applies the funds received in the course of its exchange operations to redeem a part of the Government securities in the hands of the banks, there is nothing to prevent the banks granting an equal amount of fresh credits to traders as fast as the redemption proceeds. Unless this is prevented, either by an agreed limitation of credit or by some other means, the inflation will continue unabated, and the operations of the Government will have no practical effect save to substitute a debt to Americans for a debt to British subjects. Nevertheless, this does not mean that the regulation of the exchanges is a futile measure. Provided care is taken that the sums received are applied to the reduction of credits, it is much easier to prevent the credits so cancelled being replaced by new credits, than it would be to reduce the volume of credits by direct pressure on traders. If the Government took no steps to redeem the bankers' holdings of War Loan, the deflation of credits could only be effected by one or both of the other two methods, a restriction of accommodation to individual traders or a high bank rate. Moreover, it must be remembered that if early measures are taken, the problem will be not so much how to reduce the existing inflation, as how to prevent the fresh credits demanded for restarting trade producing a further inflation. If the Government regulates the exchanges, and applies all the sums received in exchange for foreign credits to the redemption of the bankers' Government securities, the effect will be practically to substitute the new trade credits for a part of the banks' holdings of War Loan, without further swelling the banks' balance sheets. It will be easy to check a further creation of credits, in the normal way, by the operation of the bank rate, without the bank rate ever being raised in a sensational or oppressive way, perhaps without its being raised at all.

It should be observed that equally satisfactory results would be attained if the Government raised money at home for the extinction of the banks' securities ; this would sacrifice the advantage of basing the whole plan on the foreign exchanges, which supply an automatic index of its success, but would probably gain the advantage of borrowing on more favourable terms. It is commonly expected that at the end of the war we shall be compelled to borrow from abroad for the purposes of "reconstruction." It is by no means certain that this will be so. The rapidity with which our fixed capital can be renewed is limited by the amount of plant and labour that can be applied to the purpose. Before the war we were exporting an enormous portion of our investible savings, and it seems not unlikely that it will be all we can do to spend the whole of our own savings fruitfully at home. We may even have a surplus for investment abroad from the very beginning. But even if on balance we are a lending rather than a borrowing nation, we shall nevertheless for some time borrow abroad as well as lend, and therefore a regulation of the exchanges by the raising of credits abroad would not necessarily traverse the natural lines of flow of capital.

It might be supposed that the whole root of the inflation difficulty is to be found in the unlimited issue of currency notes, which has upset the equilibrium which has prevailed in the London money market for so many years. But as already pointed out, this does not affect the practice of the Bank of

England in dealing with a foreign demand for gold. Moreover, both the foreign demand for gold and the domestic demand for legal tender are only *symptoms* of an excessive creation of credits. The raising of the bank rate has some slight direct effect on the foreign exchanges, but its real efficacy as a remedy is derived from the consequent contraction of credits. High interest deters borrowers. This remedy can be applied just as effectively whether the internal circulation be gold or paper.

In point of fact the issue of currency notes contributes to prevent the particular form of inflation which we are specially concerned to guard against, the depreciation of sterling in comparison with foreign gold currencies. The notes have displaced gold, which has become available for export and has helped to depreciate the world-value of gold. If we had retained sovereigns, the quantity of gold in circulation and reserve in the United States and elsewhere would have been so much less; the value of dollars in commodities would have been correspondingly greater; and correspondingly greater also would have been the difficulty of maintaining the value of sterling. In time of war there would have been incidental advantages, provided the difficulties were surmounted and the value of sterling in gold successfully maintained, since world prices would have been lower, and we should have had to raise less money for the war. But when peace is made, and the Government is paying interest and redeeming debt instead of spending money, there is a positive advantage in keeping down the value of gold, since this will diminish the burden of our gold debt, besides facilitating the maintenance of the gold value of sterling. It will therefore probably be inadvisable to take any heroic measures to restore the circulation of sovereigns. Much must depend on the action of foreign Governments. On the one hand our present allies and enemies will soon be taking steps to put their paper currencies on a gold basis, either at the former gold par, or at a new and lower one. They could effect this without holding very large gold reserves, but in practice they are likely to start accumulating gold as soon as they can. Neutrals, on the other hand, have received during the war more gold than they can easily digest, and they will be able to part with some without suffering any contraction either of their circulating medium or of credits. This will furnish a supply of surplus gold, to which can be added the world's production of some £90,000,000 a year or more.

III.

THE GOLD STANDARD.[1]

WHEN we speak of a monetary standard we mean that which regulates the value or purchasing power of the monetary unit. The monetary unit is the unit for the measurement of debts. A debt is an economic relation which requires to be expressed as a number or quantity, and, in order that it may be so expressed, it must be expressed in terms of some unit.

Now the subject matter of debts is wealth. They arise out of transactions in wealth, and are extinguished by transactions in wealth. A sale of goods or a service rendered makes a debtor and a creditor. The debtor can extinguish his obligations, the creditor can satisfy his claims, by another sale of goods or service rendered. Such goods and services are wealth, and have value. The unit for the measurement of debts must be a unit for the measurement of values.

The monetary standard is therefore commonly called, and quite rightly called, the standard of value. But it is a mistake to suppose that it is *merely* a standard of value, no more than a unit for the comparison of different items of wealth. Such a standard of comparison would be in itself something conventional and non-essential, for, so long as the same unit were chosen within the limits of each comparison, it would not matter what the unit might be, or whether different units were used for different comparisons.

Debts, on the other hand, are the very foundation of the economic system, and the existence of a network of debts, calculated in a certain unit, is an important and substantial fact. The true function of the monetary standard is so to regulate the unit in which debts are measured as to maintain

[1] Read before Section F of the British Association, 12th September, 1919.

the stability of that system. Prices, which measure the value of commodities in terms of the unit, and inversely therefore the value of the unit in terms of commodities, are themselves potential debts. The quotation of a price is an offer, the acceptance of which completes a contract and gives rise to a debt.

The characteristic of the ideal unit for the measurement of debts is that it should have the same meaning when the debt is discharged as when it is contracted. A merchant orders a consignment of goods from a manufacturer in October to be delivered in January at an agreed price. The merchant must be able to rely on selling the goods through the retailers to the consumers at approximately the prices he anticipated ; the manufacturer must be able to rely on producing them at approximately the cost estimated.

An investor pays down a capital sum of £1000 in exchange for a perpetual annuity of £50. He wants to be able to count on £50 continuing for an indefinite period to represent the same command of wealth as when he made the investment.

A man starts work on Monday under agreement to receive £3 on Saturday. All around him commodities and services are on offer at prices with which he and his employer are both more or less familiar. In order that the bargain may be carried out in fact as well as in name, these commodities and services must be on offer at substantially the same prices on the Saturday as on the Monday.

This last, it may be said, is at any rate a modest enough demand. Prices may vary widely in a lifetime; they may vary materially in three months ; surely any variation in a week in the general level of prices must be for practical purposes negligible. But in reality wage agreements are especially a source of difficulty when the monetary standard becomes unreliable. Wages cannot be revised every week ; when the purchasing power of the monetary unit varies, they have to be altered at the cost, it may be, of grave friction, whenever the accumulated effect of the variation makes itself felt. Instability of wages means instability of the whole social system.

The seeker after an ideal monetary standard is met at the very outset by a theoretical difficulty. What he wants to secure is that a given debt shall represent, in some sense, an invariable command over wealth. But the relative values of different kinds of wealth are themselves always varying. If the unit represents the same command over one kind of wealth, it will vary in relation to another. Averages and index numbers will give an approximate test of general purchasing power, but at the best will contain an arbitrary element.

The gold standard represents a rough and ready solution of the problem; it fixes the price of one commodity. The monetary unit is equated to a prescribed quantity of the selected commodity. This commodity is a material so durable as to be almost indestructible, and one of which therefore the accumulated stocks are very large in proportion to the annual fresh supply. Gold tends, therefore, to have a remarkably steady value.

In order to make the gold standard effective, it is ordained that every debt above a certain limit shall be payable, if the creditor wishes, in gold. This system can only work if the debtor, when so required, can readily obtain the necessary quantity of gold. But of course a *solvent* debtor is himself actually or potentially a creditor, and is thus in a position to exercise the same right as his own creditor. If gold is in circulation in the form of coin, people will keep enough of it in hand to meet their liabilities. And with a banking system, of course, the banker makes it his business to supply so much gold as his customers require for their daily business, and keeps a stock in hand for the purpose.

But to maintain an effective gold standard, it is not necessary to confine the currency system to gold coin and credits payable in gold. The actual legal medium of payment may be partly or even wholly paper money or over-valued token silver. The monetary unit may none the less be kept at a fixed gold value either by the direct convertibility of the paper or tokens into gold, or by convertibility into foreign credits which are maintained at a fixed gold value, or by a mere limitation of supply so that, though inconvertible, they circulate alongside gold coin, or, theoretically at any rate, by a judicious limitation of supply based on a careful watching of the gold market.

By a combination of these systems the gold standard was in nearly universal operation at the outbreak of war in 1914. Some countries were using unregulated paper ; but it was universally recognised that paper money ought to be put on a gold basis as soon as possible. China almost alone adhered to the old silver standard. With these exceptions it was possible everywhere to exchange credits for gold and gold for credits at a fixed price, subject at the most to a fractional commission of almost negligible amount. Thus gold was an international currency.

The gold standard, in fact, gave uniformity to the monetary unit, not only in time, but in space too. A trader could with confidence exchange a credit in his own country, not only for a future credit in the same place, but for a credit, present or future, in almost any other part of the world. In peace time the portability of gold is such that, unless there are legal restrictions on its movement, its value can only differ very slightly in different places at the same time, and its world value remained steady enough from year to year for it to be accepted without reservation as the basis of financial contracts extending far into the future.

This is the system that existed before the war. The war has destroyed it. Under the strain of war finance, the Governments of Europe, unable to raise the means of payment by taxation and by genuine loans, have been driven to pay their way with paper money or with bank credits created for the purpose. In each country the plethora of credit and money has caused a fall in the purchasing power of the monetary unit, corresponding to the financial strain. The device of steadying the unit by fixing the price of one commodity has broken down, gold has vanished from circulation, and the interchangeability of credits for gold and gold for credits has for all practical purposes ceased. During the actual continuance of the war there had ceased to be a world market for gold.

4 *

The displacement of gold from circulation, along with the suspension of the demand for fresh supplies of gold for currency purposes in Europe, has thrown enormous stocks of gold upon the American market, where alone, except for some neutral countries of secondary importance, gold has continued to be used. The release of these redundant supplies has depressed the value of gold itself in comparison with other commodities. It has, in fact, enabled America, North and South, to indulge in a currency inflation not much less extravagant than that in, at any rate, the more cautious European States. Now that the war is over, it is in America that the first signs of the re-establishment of a gold market and a gold standard are to be seen. But the American market is still saturated with the excessive supplies sent thither during the war, and the purchasing power of gold remains far below the pre-war level.

This decline in the purchasing power of gold has disclosed a weakness in the gold standard. The stability in the value of gold depends on the accumulated stocks being large in proportion to the annual supply. But just because the stocks are large the quantity in use as currency is large. The demand for gold as currency, by withdrawing this large quantity from other uses, tends to keep the value of gold up. But if a great part of the demand is destroyed by the adoption of paper money in place of gold, the supplies set free are great in proportion to the world's industrial demand, and have to be absorbed as currency in the area in which gold continues to be used for that purpose. The more restricted this area, the more marked will be the effect on the value of gold. At the present time gold prices have fully doubled, or in other words, the value of gold in relation to commodities has been halved.

Except in the rapidity with which it has occurred, this phenomenon is not altogether without precedent. In 1873 silver lost the privilege, which it had shared with gold, of free interchangeability with credits. The consequent displacement of silver from use as currency only occurred gradually, but by the time the process was completed the gold value of silver had fallen from 60d. to 22d. an ounce. During the Napoleonic Wars, though the use of paper money was by no means so universal in Europe as it is now, specie prices nevertheless rose 60 per cent. above the pre-war average, and by 1822, when the use of gold and silver was restored, had fallen again to their former level.

Thus in considering the future monetary standard, we have two distinct problems to deal with. First, throughout Europe, except in Spain, the monetary units are depreciated in varying degrees in comparison with their nominal gold parities. Secondly, gold itself has lost its former stability of value.

Evidently, what we want is to regain a standard which will not vary appreciably either in time or in space. The unit must continue in the future to represent as nearly as may be the same amount of wealth as in the present; the unit of each country must bear a constant proportion to the unit of every other. This condition of things had been secured—not perfectly, but well enough to meet practical requirements—by the gold standard in 1914. Is it to be secured again by a restoration of the gold standard? (Before embarking upon the consideration of this question, let me remark parenthetically that I do not propose to deal with the interesting alternative of a return to bimetallism.)

The currency units of the European belligerents have all been depreciated, some more, some less, below their nominal gold value. To restore them to their nominal gold value, even though this means far less than their pre-war value in terms of commodities, would therefore require a measure of what may be called deflation.

Deflation is the process of restoring the value of a depreciated currency unit, or, more generally, of raising the value of the unit. In currency theory it is fundamental, and much turns on the difficulties which arise in carrying it into effect.

Inflation takes shape in an increase in the aggregate of money incomes. The rise of prices, which is its best recognised characteristic, may be regarded as the consequence of an increase in purchasing power, accompanied by no corresponding increase in the supply of things to be purchased. Deflation is a reversal of this process; it must mean a decrease in the aggregate of money incomes,

The normal instrument of deflation is an increase in the rate of interest on short-period indebtedness. The immediate effect of this measure is to deter traders from holding stocks of commodities with borrowed money. They reduce stocks in two ways. They endeavour to accelerate their sales, and therefore reduce the prices charged to the consumer. They give fewer orders to producers for the replenishment of stocks. The result is a fall of prices, and a diminution of output. And the consequent decline of profits, growth of unemployment and reduction of wages bring about just that decrease in incomes which is required.

Of course where the State is the principal short-period debtor this method requires some modification. It is no use the State trying to deter itself from borrowing by allowing its creditors a high rate of interest, and it cannot reduce its indebtedness, as a trader does, by unloading stocks. It must raise money by taxation or by genuine loans, drawn from the savings of the community, and must apply the proceeds not to expenditure but to the cancellation of redundant credits. This is in reality a direct attack on incomes. The money raised by tax and loan represents a diminution of the consumers' spending power, and therefore of the effective demand for commodities and investments.

Deflation then seems practicable enough. But its very effectiveness is an obstacle. Traders and business men have a deadly fear of dear money, and this fear is not to be explained as an exaggerated dislike of paying an extra 2 or 3 per cent. per annum for a period perhaps of much less than a year. It is a dread of the consequences which experience has shown to follow from a diminution of the money income of the country; the depreciation of assets in comparison with liabilities, and the fall of prices, which is perpetually turning a profit into a loss—these are the consequences which assail the prosperity of every one and threaten the actual solvency of those who trade with borrowed money.

And deflation also inevitably involves a reduction of wages. This is an indispensable condition both of the reduction of cost of production and of the reduction of effective demand. When money wages are too high in proportion to the supply of money, general unemployment supervenes. This unemployment must be cured either by a reduction of wages, or by an increase in the supply of money—in other words, by renewed inflation.

It is hardly necessary to enlarge on the difficulties and dangers of adjusting wages to an unstable monetary unit. We have lately had only too much experience of the process of raising wages every few months to keep pace with a depreciating currency. The contrary process of putting down wages in proportion to an appreciating currency is not likely to be less harassing. But if the gold standard is the only practicable means of steadying the value of the monetary unit, these very difficulties are the best argument for returning to it. By facing a period of tribulation we can get back to a sound currency, and shall reap our reward in having a clear future before us. The depreciation of sterling in comparison with American dollars, which are at par with gold, is serious but is not yet such as to demand an impossible effort to bridge the gap. But England is not alone in having to face this problem. Other European currencies are far more depreciated. This is shown even by the foreign exchanges, and in some cases the effect on the foreign exchanges is largely masked by a drastic restriction of imports. For some countries deflation by the methods just described would be too great a task to attempt.

There are, however, at least two methods of cutting the knot. One is to enact that the depreciated paper money shall pass at something less than its face value in terms of the monetary unit; the other is to fix the value of the monetary unit in gold at something less than the former parity. By either method the monetary unit can at a single stroke be given a legal value in gold. Both methods, however, are open to the imputation that public faith is not kept.

The first method, the reduction of the legal value of the paper money, is not only a breach of faith, in that it disappoints the expectations of those who have received the money at its old value, in many cases from the Government itself; it also concentrates all the burdens of deflation in a single day. If there is any considerable body of trade indebtedness outstanding, the effect on the position of the debtors is so calamitous that the method must be ruled out as impracticable. It can only be faced in a community where trade and credit operations have been reduced to such a low ebb that the outstanding indebtedness is negligible.

The second method, the adoption of a reduced metallic value for the monetary unit, was common in the Middle Ages. With the development of credit it has come to be regarded as illegitimate, in that it inflicts an injustice on creditors and in particular enables the State to lighten the burden of its own debts. But if the State has not the financial strength to restore the monetary unit to its old gold value, this measure may be the only alternative to the continuance of an unsupported paper standard for generation after generation. It is almost certain that some of the nations of Europe will have to resort to it.

Such, then, are the steps by which the gold standard is to be regained. The choice is between a long and painful deflation and an arbitrary manipulation of the currency, which is hardly consistent with the preservation of public good faith.

But we have not yet come to the end of the difficulties in the way. We have already observed that the displacement of vast quantities of gold from circulation in Europe has greatly depressed the world value of gold in relation to commodities. Suppose that in a few years' time the gold standard is restored to practically universal use. If the former currency systems are revived, and with them the old demands for gold, both for circulation in coin and for reserves against note issues, the value of gold in terms of commodities will go up. In proportion as it goes up, the difficulty of regaining or maintaining the gold standard will be accentuated. In other words, if the countries which are striving to recover the gold standard compete with one another for the existing supply of gold, they will drive up the world-value of gold, and will find themselves burdened with a much more severe task of deflation than they ever anticipated.

And at the present time the situation is complicated by
the portentous burden of the national debts. Except for
America and this country, none of the principal participants
in the war can see clearly the way to solvency. Even we,
with taxation at war level, can only just make ends meet.
France, Italy, Germany, and Belgium have hardly made a
beginning with the solution of their financial problems. The
higher the value of the monetary unit in which one of these
vast debts is calculated, the greater will be the burden on the
taxpayers responsible for it. The effect of inflation in swelling
the nominal national income is clearly demonstrated by the
British income tax returns, and by the well-sustained consumption of dutiable commodities notwithstanding enormous
increases in the rates of duty. Deflation decreases the money
yield of the revenue, while leaving the money burden of the
debt undiminished. Deflation also, it is true, diminishes the
expenses of Government, and when the debt charges are small
in proportion to the rest, it does not greatly increase the
national burdens. But now that the debt charge itself is our
main pre-occupation, we may find the continuance of some
degree of inflation a necessary condition of solvency.

Financial strain is indeed the main obstacle to currency
reform. During the war it was financial strain that produced
inflation. But the emergency measures of the war postponed
a part of the financial strain, and, now that we have to balance
our budgets, the problem has become more formidable even
than during the war. Suppose that the financial strain in one
of these overburdened communities reaches breaking-point,
where will this breaking-point be found? What will be its
symptoms, and what will be its consequences. The immediate
symptom will be a failure to balance the budget ; a deficit will
appear that cannot be bridged by additions to taxes which
are already oppressive and inelastic. Loans which, if successful, would but increase the future burdens, will be under-
subscribed, like Necker's loans of 1789. The deficit is covered
by the creation of bank credits and the printing of paper
money. This is not in itself necessarily fatal. It is a question
of degree. It may be that in a few years the monetary unit

will find a depreciated level at which solvency becomes again possible, and it can then be linked up with foreign currencies at a new parity.   But every abortive attempt at settling the unit is a source of danger.   The critical point is reached when people cease to rely on the value of money and of rights to receive money.   The Government having tried to establish the value of the monetary unit and having failed, distrust of the unit shows itself in a general desire to get rid of balances of money or credit in exchange for commodities or for gold or for foreign currencies.   So the distrust itself accentuates the depreciation, and of course the depreciation accentuates the distrust.   It is in such conditions that trade is brought to a standstill by the sheer want of any tolerable medium of exchange.   Transactions cannot be carried through, because there is no unit in which debts can be measured.   For the last two years we have seen communities starving, not because there was no food, but because the peasants and farmers would not sell food for paper money.   In Revolutionary France, when the Constituent Assembly failed to sustain the assignats, producers and traders eventually insisted, despite the law, on being paid in metallic currency.   The consequent demand for gold and silver shook the whole credit system of the world. For the moment Eastern Europe seems to have submitted to economic paralysis; no medium of exchange has taken the place of the hopelessly discredited rouble; the mark and the crown are on the verge of collapse.   Conceivably some or all of these currencies, instead of being restored to stability, may be cleared away along with all the debts and credits based upon them, and the economic system of Eastern Europe may have to be begun afresh with a metallic medium of exchange drained away from the West.

It cannot, therefore, be assumed that the failure of some countries to restore a gold standard by currency legislation and the control of credit will relieve the demand for gold in the rest.   It may on the contrary intensify the demand, and this is a danger for which we ought to be prepared.

These problems illustrate that weak point of the gold standard, to which we have already alluded.   The value of gold is only steady so long as the demand for it as currency remains substantially unchanged. If we are going to adhere to the gold standard in future, it is most desirable that the absorption of gold for currency purposes should everywhere be kept in control. If all the principal countries of the world settle in the near future what the value of their currency units in gold is to be, we want so to regulate the demand for gold that the value of these currency units in commodities does not vary substantially. To achieve this result it will be necessary to retain the present proportion of gold to credit and paper money taken in the aggregate in all the countries, except so far as the amount of credit and paper money may be reduced by deflation in the interval before the gold standard is established. There will therefore have to be a very great economy in the use of gold as compared with what prevailed before the war. Modern refinements in the regulation of currencies make this possible. By the gold exchange standard, which has become the favourite of currency theorists, it is possible to maintain the monetary unit of a country at par with the unit of a gold-using country, without the former absorbing any gold at all. It is not necessary for the Western European countries to go to this length and dispense with gold altogether, for they have retained gold reserves of substantial amount, though in nothing like the pre-war proportion to their paper circulation. All that is required is that they shall not endeavour to add to their stocks of gold at one another's expense. And this the gold exchange standard makes possible. The principal bank of issue in each country must be willing to offer credits or paper money in exchange for credits or paper money in any other, on terms just favourable enough to compete successfully with the import of gold.

But if this system is well calculated to prevent an excessive demand for gold as currency, it is open to the contrary danger that it may allow an almost indefinite expansion of paper money with a fixed substructure of gold reserves. The only counteracting influence would be the demand for gold in industry, but the value of gold in relation to other commodities will have to fall a long way before the industrial demand is so far stimulated as even to absorb the annual new production from the mines, let alone to make any impression on the vast amount of the world's accumulated reserves. The tendency of credit, if left to itself, to expand indefinitely makes this a very real danger, though the consequences are not so oppressive as those of an undue appreciation of the monetary units. A persistent depreciation of the monetary unit not only upsets the balance between debtor and creditor, but means a corresponding rise in the cost of living and necessitates those perpetual revisions of wages which we have already had occasion to mention.

We seek, in fact, a middle course. We want to use the gold exchange standard to dispense each country from absorbing gold when it needs additional currency, and at the same time we want to prevent any country from abusing this arrangement to increase its currency circulation unduly. The scientific economist will be tempted to look for a solution in the regulation of currencies by index numbers of prices. Probably something can be done in this direction. The practical legislator would indeed hesitate to define the value of the monetary unit in terms of an index number, and even the scientific economist must admit that there are many practical difficulties in the system, which have not yet been solved. The function of the index number will be rather to give guidance, along with other data, in the administrative control of currency, than to play a part in the mechanical rigidity of a statutory system.

But it will probably be thought dangerous to trust entirely to administrative discretion, and the best form for a legislative regulation of the currency to take is a direct limitation on the quantity of paper money. The limit may be placed either on the proportion of the total issue to the metallic reserve, or on the total uncovered issue. The former system is often recommended on the ground of its elasticity, but this elasticity is a very equivocal advantage, for in proportion as the system facilitates expansion it makes contraction more difficult and dangerous. The maximum uncovered issue is really the more practical and workable plan.

Whatever system is adopted must be the subject of international agreement. If the pitfalls are to be avoided, if the world-value of gold is to be stabilised, there will be an arbitrary or conventional factor in the currency problem, which no individual state will be able to evaluate without reference to its neighbours.

The basis of this international agreement will be the establishment by each of the participating States of a currency law calculated to allow so much uncovered paper money as, with the portion covered by gold, will just provide for its needs, with a suitable margin or reserve left over. This margin or reserve (like the banking reserve of the Bank of England) is necessary to allow of the inevitable casual and seasonal variations. The supply of currency of each country must be, as nearly as may be, such that all the foreign exchanges are at or near their new gold parities. Once this state of equilibrium has been attained it must be preserved by the gold exchange standard.

The gold exchange standard may be applied in more than one way. The usual practice is to offer to buy or sell credits abroad in exchange for credits at home, a reserve of foreign bills or other foreign assets being maintained, to be drawn upon for the purpose. These foreign assets are sometimes counted as the equivalent of a gold reserve for the purposes of the currency law. Clearly this must not be allowed. And if the gold exchange standard is to reproduce as nearly as possible the gold movements that would occur under a simple gold system, what is wanted is not an exchange of credits but an exchange of legal tender money—that is to say, anyone with legal tender money in one country should be able to surrender it in exchange for an equivalent amount of legal tender money in any other country, the amount so surrendered being withdrawn from circulation. In fact, this would mean that any country, party to the agreement, could add to the paper money based in accordance with its currency law on the gold reserve, further issues based on reserves of foreign paper money placed in its hands abroad. These additional issues being equal to the reserves held against them, the aggregate circulation of paper money in the international system would remain unchanged, and would still be limited in accordance with the aggregate gold reserves.

Any country which indulged in inflation, or allowed its currency unit to depreciate, would find more and more of its paper money locked up in the exchange reserves and withdrawn from circulation. This would operate like the export of gold.

If legal tender money were the sole means of payment the system would work automatically. The mere scarcity of currency would itself restrict purchases and bring about a reduction of prices. But the principal means of payment in modern business is credit. Credit is only transformed into legal tender money for the payment of wages and for the smaller transactions. A scarcity of legal tender money does not affect prices until it has reacted on credit. As the possessor of a bank credit is free to draw as much of it as he pleases in cash, the first impact of the scarcity is felt entirely by the banks and not at all by the public. This is a signal to the banks to contract credits, and its effectiveness depends on their responding to the signal.

To rely exclusively on a regulation of the legal tender currency is therefore fallacious. Far from solving the problem of controlling the currency, it merely passes on to the bankers the burden of solving it.

And that is the reason for proposing, besides the limitation of uncovered paper money and the gold exchange standard, the use of an index number of prices in the administrative control of currency. If we rely on the limitation of paper money, and the bankers do not succeed in keeping control of credit, the inevitable result will be that, when the bank reserves in some or all countries threaten to melt away to nothing, the limitation of paper money will be suspended.

Credit has an inherent tendency to expand, and the problem of controlling it reduces itself in practice to curbing this tendency in time to prevent undue depreciation of the monetary unit. Essentially depreciation means a rise in the average level of prices, and therefore the index number of prices affords the most direct measure of the movements to be counteracted. And what is more important still, the rise of prices *precedes* the drain of legal tender money into circulation. It will be the function of the principal banks of issue of the associated States to watch the index of world prices, and to put the brake on by raising the rate of interest as soon as a material rise is recorded. But this must not be done without discrimination. On the one hand, a rise of prices may be due not to credit expansion but to a scarcity of one or two important commodities. On the other, an incipient expansion of credit may take effect not in a rise of prices but in an increased volume of purchases. The banking authorities must take into account not only the statistical data, such as the index numbers, but also all that they can learn of the state of business from their relations with traders.

Regulating credit, in fact, is an exceedingly delicate operation. How, then, it may be asked, can we hope to arrive at a system of international control? Most of the countries co-operating will be subjected for many years to come to prodigious financial burdens. The power of inflating credit or over-issuing paper money is intimately connected with Government finance, and in the last resort may afford the only alternative to an act of bankruptcy. A Government will not definitely divest itself of this power, nor, if it did, could its undertaking be in all circumstances observed. Are we to expect the development of a delicately balanced international mechanism from a crowd of distracted financiers, each preoccupied with the desperate embarrassments of his country and ready to clutch at any expedient to gain a few months' respite from his troubles? Or are we first going to assume that all the real difficulties of the situation have been surmounted, and then tell the world what sort of currency system will be best for it?

The answer is that in practice the effectiveness of an international system would not absolutely depend on its universality. The very moment British currency is re-established on a gold basis, and sterling and dollars are at par, a beginning can be made. The United Kingdom and the United

States, together with a number of minor powers, which have acquired large gold reserves and considerable financial strength during the war, could start the system. An Anglo-American combination would command so large a proportion of the world's stock of gold that it would be almost sufficient by itself. The mere existence of so important a currency system on a stable basis would lead other countries to regulate their own monetary units by it, even though they never bound themselves by any agreement. When a collapse of credit precipitates an intense demand for a metallic currency, that is because there is no other medium of payment that people will trust or recognise. If there is a foreign credit system, which can be made the basis of a new currency, it will be easier to utilise this through an exchange system than to import gold.

Again, leaving aside the danger of an actual currency collapse, the financially weaker countries have less power of attracting gold. If the financially strong are in the combination, then, however great the gold hunger of the remainder may be, its effect on the world-value of gold will be relatively moderate. Nor are the financially weaker countries likely to let loose their stocks of gold to flood the market. Indeed, except in the case of France, the gold holdings of these countries are hardly great enough to flood the market, and France is always intensely reluctant to part with gold.

In reality, therefore, we can arrive at a fairly satisfactory practical solution of our currency problems as soon as we can reach an arrangement between England and America, with a view to maintaining their aggregate uncovered paper issues as nearly as possible at a fixed amount, to providing for remittances between them on a gold exchange basis, and to controlling credit with a view to keeping the gold value of commodities, as measured by an index number, approximately constant. The third of these conditions is the most novel, but, if it could be carried into effect, would be the most useful. It might not be consistent with the first, but where they differ it would, at any rate in theory, be the more correct guide to follow, and the paper currency law could be adjusted from time to time as might be necessary.

The purpose of such a system would be not merely to restore the gold standard, but to make it a more trustworthy standard than it has been in the past. The demand for gold as currency would, in fact, be so regulated as to make the value of a gold unit itself in commodities as nearly as possible constant.

IV.

THE EUROPEAN CURRENCY SITUATION.[1]

TWO years ago, when Europe was first emerging from war, such ominous cracks began to appear in the economic structure that more than one observer was tempted to say that the credit system of the Continent was about to collapse. Western Europe has up to now been preserved from the fulfilment of that prediction. But collapse is not too strong a word to describe the financial condition of the States into which the peoples formerly included in the three Empires of Germany, Russia, and Austria-Hungary have been redistributed.

The shortest way to express what has happened to Eastern Europe is to say that the money of account has lost stability and forfeited confidence. The primary causes of this catastrophe are so well known that there is no need to elaborate them. Let it suffice to say that the burden of war budgets far exceeded the resources of the belligerent Governments from tax or loan; that, to find the means of payment to cover the deficiency, there was nothing left but the issue of more and more paper money, with or without the thin disguise of borrowing from a central bank of issue; finally, that the consequent superabundance of the means by which debts are legally payable has struck at the root of the value of the debts themselves. Public opinion has everywhere made progress, especially since the Brussels Conference, in understanding both the disease and the remedy. The first necessity of the distressed countries is, as we all know, to balance their budgets. Their distresses arose from budget deficits, and will remain so long as the deficits continue. Once the new issues of paper money are stopped, the rest will be easy; many

[1] Written in January, 1921.

66

valuable measures can be devised to help credit on its way to recovery, but they count for little in comparison with this one paramount need.

But even though the original cause and the ultimate remedy be so clearly seen, it is still worth while to analyse with some care the consequences to human society of so fundamental an economic disaster as a collapse of the monetary unit of account. In economic reasoning short cuts are dangerous; an apparently legitimate transition may mean the disregard of an essential link in the chain. And when it comes to devising practical remedies, all the circumstances must be taken into account. In what follows we shall endeavour to elucidate in some detail the manner in which the breakdown in credit machinery has affected the economic life of Eastern Europe. Our investigation will not apply to any one country ; it will be true in varying degrees of all. And some of the symptoms are recognisable in a less severe form in Western Europe also.

Value is a relation, and the value of a monetary unit can only be expressed as a relation between it and the various forms of wealth. A price expresses the value of a commodity relative to the unit, and the value of the unit relative to a commodity is expressed by the inverse of a price. A fall in the value of the unit is therefore measured by a rise in the prices of all commodities, and not only of all commodities, but in the prices of services, that is to say in wages, fees, and salaries, and in the prices of foreign currencies, that is to say, in the foreign exchanges.

But one of the most striking characteristics of the monetary collapse in Eastern Europe is that, though the value of the unit has fallen, prices have risen very unequally. No consistent measure can be found of the proportional depreciation of the unit, because different commodities give measures so divergent that they do not even yield a significant average. In Germany, for example, one commodity may be at fifty times its pre-war price, another at five times. Wages, house rents, and the foreign exchanges exhibit similar variations. The same is true of the other countries.

5 *

The issue of redundant paper money does not necessarily in the first instance raise prices. Its *immediate* effect is rather to hasten sales. The people to whom the paper money is first paid have more to spend, while their neighbours have as much to spend as before. Between them they buy more than they did, consumption is increased, and the traders' stocks of commodities are diminished. Traders are almost more pleased to sell quickly than to sell at high prices, and it is only when their stocks are reduced inconveniently low that they begin to raise their prices.

Inflation of the currency therefore has a direct tendency to cause *scarcity*, quite apart from any adverse effect it may have on production, because it depletes the accumulated stocks of commodities. The rise of prices, when it comes, is merely the traders' defence against this tendency. They put up prices to preserve their stocks from complete annihilation. During the war, in the belligerent countries, production for any but war-like purposes was severely curtailed; in Eastern Europe importation was reduced almost to nothing. Even without currency troubles, the insistent demand of the consumers, pressing upon inadequate supplies, would have necessitated a rise of prices. But so great a rise of prices as was threatened would have meant acute distress for the main body of the population, and the belligerent Governments hastened to prescribe maximum prices. Yet this was to take away the traders' defence against the depletion of their stocks. Hence there followed the rationing of supplies.

So long as the war lasted, prices were artificially kept down, and stocks were protected, not with complete success, by rationing. This meant that the people who received paper money did not have adequate opportunities of spending it. In so far as they could be induced to subscribe the money they saved to War Loans (almost the only form of investment then open to them) the redundancy was diminished. But it is characteristic of a period of inflation that investments yielding a fixed rate of interest become unattractive. The greatest prospect of profit is held out by the purchase of commodities, to be resold at higher prices, or by investment in industrial securities, which are expected to reflect the high profits on the commodities to be produced.

The war-time obstacles to production, import, and sale did not entirely counteract this tendency. Even though willing sellers at the maximum prices could not be found, or the sources of supply were dried up during the war, it was still worth while to keep an accumulation of cash idle, yet available for immediate use in trade, rather than lock it up in Government securities, which might become unrealisable at the critical moment.

Thus at the end of 1918 there existed in Eastern Europe a vast flood of paper money temporarily dammed up by artificial economic restrictions. The situation in Western Europe was less perilous. Having greater financial strength to begin with, the Entente Powers had had all the resources of the world to draw upon, and in the end had received the potent economic support of the United States.

For Eastern Europe the end of the war meant not only defeat and revolution, but an economic *sauve qui peut.* Though war-time restrictions for the most part were, at any rate nominally, continued, it was no longer possible to enforce them effectively. The dam gave way, and the flood of paper money poured out. It poured out, but into what channels? Prices, wages, profits, salaries having been artificially kept down, the national income had not risen in proportion to the stock of currency. From the point of view of the individual, his balance of cash was greater than his circumstances required. This was especially so in the case of the trader, who had turned much of his working capital into cash by selling off commodities which he could not replace, but in many cases it was true of the private person, who would have liked to buy clothes, furniture, good food, and other comforts and luxuries during the war, but could not procure them. With the return of peace, the possessors of this excessive stock of paper money sought to exchange it for commodities. But the commodities were not there, and production could not be revived for want of materials.

The demand alike for completed products and for materials,

in a country so situated, could only be satisfied from abroad, and thither the torrent of paper money turned. It beat against the foreign exchange market, but here it could not break through. The only effect of the pressure was to force up the prices of foreign currencies ever higher and higher. The intense demand for commodities could only find relief from foreign countries in so far as the country could offer something in exchange for their products. In other words, if every one was buying foreign currencies, and no one selling them, the market would become nominal, and no business could be done. Apart from convertibility into gold, the currency of a country possesses value as being the legal means of paying for its products. If the country is in such a state of distress that it can spare no products for export, foreign dealers will only buy its currency with a view to future gain. They may either buy some of the paper currency itself, or they may acquire a bank deposit, or they may lend money in the country repayable at a future date. The possible fluctuations in the exchange are so great that the question whether interest is payable becomes one of little consequence; the transaction is to all intents and purposes a speculation in exchange. In 1919 there was a good deal of this speculative acquisition of marks, crowns, and other European currencies. This was by no means confined to speculative purchases by dealers in exchange; it included much speculative holding of sums received in the course of trade by dealers in commodities. Both the dealers in commodities and the dealers in exchange seemed to think that the depreciation, great as it was even then, was a temporary aberration from the old gold parity. When marks were worth, say, 5 cents or 3d., it seemed attractive to buy them and ruinous to sell them, even if several years had to pass before they returned to their pre-war value of 23·8 cents, or 11¾d.

But in any market the existence of a considerable body of speculators for a rise is a source of weakness. While they are buying, they support the market, but the support comes to an end with the buying, and, as soon as they abandon the hope of a rise, their rush to sell depresses the market as much as their former rush to buy raised it.   Now the foreign exchange market in 1919 was in a peculiarly unstable condition.   No independent standard existed for assessing the intrinsic value of any of the currencies of Europe.   An economist would have advised a measurement of the average prices of commodities ; a standard based on what has come to be called the " purchasing power parity." [1]   But even he would have been baffled ; he would have found the prices of domestic products utterly at variance with one another, and all more or less artificial owing to the restrictions of law or custom; he would have found the prices of foreign commodities calculated from world prices and the actual rate of exchange.   In practice dealers in a market try so to fix prices as to equalise supply and demand.   But if the demand is *wholly* speculative, the price arrived at is meaningless.   It expresses nothing more than the opinion of the speculators, and in the case of the exchange market the very difficulty was that the speculators had no guidance in forming their opinion.   It was apparently early in 1920 that this phase of speculation in the exchanges of the distressed countries came to an end.   At any rate it was in January, 1920, that the American banks refused any longer to continue advances to exporters who were holding the proceeds of sale in European currencies.   Marks and crowns fell precipitately, and the currencies of Western Europe suffered too.   In the spring, when the pressure was over, they recovered.

But recovery, of course, was only relative.   Comparison of the exchanges on New York in June, 1920, with those a year before shows only too clearly the effect of the insistent pressure to buy, backed up by utterly insufficient real economic power.

The inexorable barrier of the foreign exchange market everywhere turned back the stream of demand from foreign to domestic commodities.   Given the free play of economic forces, unhampered by either law or custom, the prices of home products ought thereupon to have risen in the same

---

[1] This convenient phrase (which is due to Prof. Gustav Cassel—see " Economic Journal " for December, 1918) promises to be the subject of almost as much controversy as the quantitative theory of money itself.

proportion as those of foreign products in the same currency. But such freedom did not and could not exist. Even where prices were not regulated by law, retail traders were reluctant, and even ashamed to put them up to the apparently extortionate level that market conditions would bear. When, for example, the buying power of the public would in reality justify prices being quadrupled, shopkeepers who only doubled them might still be attacked as profiteers.

In the case of the necessaries of life a sudden and great increase of price seemed so dangerous in its social consequences that the Governments everywhere thought it essential to take control, or rather to retain control, over both prices and supply.

When an excessive supply of paper money has been issued, but has been prevented by obstacles, such as those which existed during the war, from exercising its full effect on incomes, the first effect of the removal of those obstacles is to increase *profits*, that is to say, the incomes of those who buy or produce commodities with a view to sale. Incomes derived from interest on securities or from rents under leases are fixed. Rents, even where not fixed by contract for the term of a lease, have been limited by law. Professional incomes from fees or salaries move slowly. Wages respond more easily to a change in circumstances, but only *after* a change in prices and profits has made itself clearly felt. The result is that a rise of prices presents itself as a severe hardship to the great majority of the people. Further, it reveals a sharp antagonism of interest between the small minority of manufacturers and merchants who make their living by dealing in commodities, and the rest. The right course, or at any rate the course recommended by orthodox political economy, would have been to let the wage-earners and salary-earners press for increased remuneration in proportion to the rise of prices, which measured both the increase in cost of living to themselves and the increase of their employers' profits.

But to that there were at least two obstacles. In the first place, wage-bargains are difficult to arrive at, and are liable to cause friction and unrest. This is so even in normal circumstances, when labour seeks to share the exceptional profits of a period of good trade, or consents to accept a reduction of wages for fear of unemployment at a time of depression. But when the monetary unit has lost stability of value, the difficulties are accentuated. Neither party to the bargain can form any clear idea of the factors which should go to make a just settlement. Cost of production depends on calculations which may be made obsolete by a variation in the currency unit in a few days. A manufacturer, in the interval between acceptance and completion of a contract, may see his neighbour getting an order at double the price he is to receive. Workmen must display great alacrity if they are to claim an addition to their wages every time a change of circumstances justifies it. Even if some of the best organised workmen get all or nearly all that the market will bear, others will certainly find their wages dropping far behind.

But in 1919 there was a second and more fundamental objection to leaving wages and prices free. Disorganisation and distress had proceeded so far that the productivity of human effort had been seriously impaired. With a large proportion of the population of Eastern Europe, it was doubtful whether the value of what they could produce would be sufficient to meet the cost of their subsistence. For them free markets for labour and for commodities would mean starvation.

Accordingly it was decided to make existence possible for the working classes, not by an increase of wages in proportion to the increased stock of currency, but by the retention of maximum prices for food and the prolongation of other war-time measures. This decision, which was by no means confined to Eastern Europe, has had far-reaching consequences. It has been accompanied by a system of fixing wages according to the cost of living. The rise in the cost of living, being based principally upon the prices of controlled articles, has been kept below and in some countries far below the rise in prices generally. Real wages have therefore been main-tained at something that may be called the subsistence level (though a terribly low level even for subsistence), while the money cost of labour has increased less in proportion than the money cost of most commodities.   But this has thrown upon the Government the responsibility of providing supplies. Supplies may be obtained either at home or from abroad. Before the war few countries in Europe were so highly industrialised as to be dependent to a serious extent upon foreign supplies of food.   But shortage of labour and shortage of fertilisers, and in some districts the devastation done by invading armies, made terrible inroads on agricultural productivity, and the opening of the year 1919 found nearly every country of Europe in urgent need of imported food supplies.

This was merely one instance of the insistent demand for commodities, which started the adverse course of the foreign exchanges.   It differed from other instances in that in each country the Government had made itself responsible for the food supply, and was the sole purchaser.   It differed also in that supplies were a matter not of choice but of necessity. The Governments, brought up against the problem of buying food without the means of paying for it, inevitably sought to borrow.   But, for reasons to which we shall refer presently, the richer countries became more and more unwilling to lend to their poorer neighbours.

When foreign loans were denied them, the distressed Governments of Europe were thrown back on the exchange market.   But whenever they entered the market, the value of their own currencies began to fall.   As we have seen, the demand for those currencies was almost purely speculative. Having no basis except the speculators' hopes of the future, this demand was easily frightened away.   That meant that the exchange started falling till it reached a point at which a new set of speculators, thinking that it must at last have touched the lowest, would buy it for a rise.   To a Government obliged to buy exchange, the speculators had the appearance of taking advantage of the national necessity to charge an exorbitant price for foreign currencies.

An unfavourable balance of trade is often put forward as the explanation of an adverse movement of the foreign exchanges.

This explanation seems to be regarded by many people as axiomatic, as if it were the one certain and universally accepted principle in a subject full of doubts and controversies. But except in a very limited sense the explanation is a fallacy. The error proceeds from the assumption that an uncovered balance of imports over exports is something *given*, to which the exchange market has to accommodate itself. As was pointed out more than a century ago by the famous Bullion Committee, an uncovered balance, an excess, that is, of indebtedness to foreign countries, is a transitory phenomenon. It is the function of an unfavourable exchange itself to redress the balance; to discourage imports and encourage exports, till the debts to and from foreign countries can be equated. If the exchange market were in perfect working order, the adjustments would be made so promptly that no appreciable uncovered balance of indebtedness in either direction would ever appear. When it does appear, it is a *symptom*, the interpretation of which is that the rate of exchange is not at the point which secures equilibrium. If the rate fails to move at once to the equilibrium point and so to obliterate the uncovered balance, that is merely because there are some creditors who are content to postpone the remittance of the sums due to them, who, in other words, are willing to speculate in exchange.

A country which can produce little may need to import much in order to save its population from starvation. An adverse balance of trade would be for it a "necessity," because without it the people cannot live. But that does not mean that we can first estimate the "necessary" amount of uncovered imports, and then suppose rates of exchange to accommodate themselves to this situation. If an adequate equivalent is not forthcoming (in the form of foreign credits or loans, where other means of payment are not available) the "necessary" imports will not come at all. The rate of exchange will become so adverse that the cash in the hands of the people will not pay the price of their necessary subsistence. They cannot live without foreign supplies, but that does not mean that they get them. They may perish.

Fundamentally the intervention of the Government does not alter this position. Its power of issuing unlimited paper money does not profit the Government at all, for the foreign seller will certainly not accept it. The Government must itself procure foreign currency.

In some cases, at any rate, recourse has been had to the compulsory requisitioning at a fixed official rate of exchange of the credits acquired in foreign countries by exporters. This expedient was tried so long ago as the sixteenth century, when Sir Thomas Gresham applied it to the Merchant Adventurers trading with Antwerp.

On the palpable futility of such a method it is hardly necessary to enlarge. It is enough to point out that the exchange market was no less injured by the diminution of the meagre supply of foreign currencies than it would have been by a corresponding addition to the demand for them, and that the purchase of these currencies at a fixed rate was equivalent to an onerous tax on that incipient export trade which it was so desirable to encourage. And in any case the amount of exchange to be collected by this method, when the export trade had hardly begun to revive, did not go far towards meeting the Government's needs. In the last resort there was no way of making good the deficiency but by paying a higher and higher price for foreign currencies.

So the burden of the unfavourable exchanges fell above all on the Governments. And the higher the price they had to pay for exchange, the greater was the budget deficit to be covered. At a time when all budgets had been stretched beyond breaking-point, an additional charge could only be met by printing more paper money. Food subsidies originating in this way have played a prominent part in the financial strain which has led to the present widespread break-down of credit. For the original accumulation of paper money that existed at the end of 1918 could have been absorbed, if only that had been the limit of the problem. It was when the accumulation was being swollen by ever-growing supplies of fresh currency that confidence was forfeited.

Loss of confidence in this connection does not mean loss

of confidence in the ability or willingness of the Government or of other people to pay their obligations. Nor does it mean loss of confidence in the acceptability of paper money in payment of debts at its nominal value. It means loss of confidence in the future purchasing power of the monetary unit itself. It means, in fact, an expectation that prices will rise.

This is a paradox. Under normal conditions, when a man of business speaks of "confidence," he usually means an expectation that prices will rise. For rising prices mean high profits and active business, and make solvency easy. But this is confidence in the value of commodities relative to money, and it is the exact contrary of confidence in the value of money relative to commodities.

At the outset, loss of confidence does not take the form of any conscious distrust of the currency. The expectation of a rise of prices operates in a perfectly normal way. It leads traders to hasten their purchases, in order to profit by the rise. This means that they turn their money into goods; they hold larger stocks of goods and smaller stocks of money. A reduction so made in holdings of money, though it appears to be a very ordinary business operation, is in reality a symptom of that loss of confidence with which we are concerned. And it has important consequences. If people are not willing to keep so much money idle in proportion to their turnover, that means that they will do a larger turnover with a given balance of idle money. And indeed, since the money one man spends is received by another, the *total* of balances is not reduced. The desire to reduce balances finds expression in an increase of business; and thereby it brings about that very increase of prices and of profits which was anticipated.

This supplies an instructive illustration of the quantity theory of money. Some would say that it constitutes an exception to the theory, but it is an exception only to that crude and long discredited form of the theory, which bases the value of the currency unit upon the quantity in circulation alone to the exclusion of other factors. Among these other factors is the relation between turnover or income and the quantity of money in circulation. The desire to reduce balances of idle money alters this relation.   It increases the " rapidity of circulation,'' and so accentuates the redundancy of the currency and raises prices, even though the amount in circulation be not increased.

The tendency to get rid of idle balances of money soon extends beyond the class of traders in commodities. It appears among dealers in foreign exchange, who, anticipating a rise in the value of foreign currencies, hasten to buy them, and part with their own currency in exchange.   It appears eventually among consumers.   To the consumer in normal times a rise or fall of prices appears as an act of fate.   Except in the case of perishable commodities, like fish or fruit, it happens only at rare intervals, and he does not try to foresee it, or to take advantage of it.   But when the currency has become unstable, and changes of price are substantial and frequent, the consumer begins to take as much interest in markets as the dealer.   The tendency to buy in anticipation of requirements spreads to him, and he likewise reduces his balances of ready money.

It may be asked, cannot this tendency to discredit be checked by a control of prices?   A control of prices as rigorous and universal as that exercised by the Jacobins in 1794 might stop the speculation in commodities.   But nothing short of a reign of terror can enforce such a control, and it is doubtful whether even a reign of terror could enforce it for long.   But even if it were enforced, what would be the result? It would become impossible to buy.   Paper money would cease to be a medium of exchange at all, and then indeed it would be discredited.   In place of the speculative tendency to lay out all available cash in the purchase of commodities, there would be a direct distrust of the currency.   This is not a mere conclusion of deductive theory.   Maximum prices have been imposed all over Europe, and, though they have been neither so universal nor so effective as under the Jacobins, they have been applied to most agricultural products, and have been enforced with sufficient rigour to govern the open market for those products.   These maximum prices are part of the system of State control of the food supply.   A Government, striving in vain to avoid forcing up the price of exchange by purchases of supplies abroad, hopes at any rate to keep its outlay on home-produced food within bounds. But in the result the hope has proved to be an illusion. The maximum price has been insufficiently attractive to the producer. He has not troubled to obtain the full yield from his land, and has preferred to consume a great part of the restricted yield at home, or to store the surplus rather than to sell it. And he has learnt to distrust the paper money in which he is paid for what he does sell, because in return for it he cannot get anything like a fair equivalent in other commodities. This distrust of paper money began in Russia in 1916. One of the greatest food-producing countries in the world was reduced to partial starvation, mainly because there was no medium of payment which would induce the peasants to produce or to part with their supplies.

Moreover, when the maximum prices apply only to a limited class of commodities, the effect is that the people, spending less on these things, have all the more to spend on the others which are not controlled. This is equally true even when the limitation of prices is not imposed by law, but is due to custom, or to the pressure of public opinion, or to the slowness of traders in taking action, or indeed to any cause except plentiful supplies. Nor is the effect confined to the case where the limitation of price applies to commodities. It follows equally from a limitation of house rents, railway fares, and even of wages.

Some wages are paid for services, such as those of domestic servants, which are rendered directly for the convenience or comfort of their employers. It is obvious that a limitation of the price of such services is closely parallel to a limitation of the price of a commodity. But even in the case of industrial wages the same principle is at work. For the employer gains what his workmen lose. Even if he forgoes the excessive profits which he is thus in a position to secure, that only means that the merchants and retailers who intervene between him and the consumer can, if they please, get the profits for themselves. If these in turn are content with less than the market will pay, then the finished commodity itself drops into the class of things limited in price, and the purchasing power so set free goes to enhance the prices of other commodities. Thus wage limitation is a particular case of price limitation, and the whole system of cheapening the necessaries of life in order to avoid an apparently exorbitant rise of wages, ends in nothing better than a vast subsidy in aid of profits at the expense of a bankrupt Government.

In one respect, however, price control may tend to counter-act the effects of loss of confidence in the currency. It inter-poses obstacles in the way of the spending of money, and so may compel people to accumulate balances. The opportunities of spending on uncontrolled commodities, even with the prospect of almost illimitable rises of price in the near future, may not prove attractive to people who are seeking in vain for supplies of urgently needed controlled commodities. But this is no mitigation of the discredit of the currency. On the contrary an accumulation of currency caused by the want of facilities for spending is a most perilous factor in the situation. Given adequate supplies, or even a break-down of control, and the accumulation is dissipated and the inflation aggravated. This, as we saw above, is what happened at the end of the war.

If the distresses of the peoples of Eastern Europe are concentrated in their Governments, that is because for the time being the play of ordinary economic motives is no longer adequate to secure the complex co-operation of effort which is necessary under modern conditions for production, distribution, and exchange. Some one must take the lead, must exercise forethought, must display initiative. No agency but the Government can fulfil this need; indeed, any other that received and exercised the requisite powers would by that very fact practically become the Government.

When the Government is in economic control, the shortage of necessary commodities from which the nation is suffering is translated into a budget deficit. Other causes contribute to the deficit. Originated by war expenditure and war debt, it is but aggravated by food subsidies. In one country the deficit is swollen by the continuance of military operations or the maintenance of excessive armaments, in another by indemnity payments, in another by the outlay on repairing the ravages of war, in another by the severance of long-established political and economic ties.

And these budget deficits are not mere symptoms. The very substance of the malady is *a want of economic power*. It is because of this want that the deficits are met by the issue of paper money; if real instead of fictitious wealth could be found to meet them, the disease would be cured.

The failure of revenue is as much the result of the want of economic power as the excess of expenditure. It arises partly from the actual shortage in the production of wealth, partly from the same disorganisation of economic machinery that causes that shortage.

For the shortage of production is traceable to the disorganisation of economic machinery. Its immediate causes may be discerned in the under-feeding of workmen, in the inadequate supplies of materials, in the breakdown of transport and plant. But these could all be cured by credit. It is the breakdown of credit that is at fault, and that breakdown proceeds from the discredit of the monetary unit.

We have seen how the discredit has come about, and what forms it takes. We have seen how inflation causes a scarcity of commodities and the scarcity of commodities intensifies the inflation; how the redundancy of paper money depresses the monetary unit and the depression of the unit brings about a greater redundancy; how the fall in its value discredits the unit and the discredit accelerates the fall. But these tendencies are distinct from the breakdown of credit itself. By credit in this connection we mean primarily the system of short-period loans by which trade is financed. Traders, whether they are manufacturers or merchants, are accustomed to supplement their own capital with borrowed money. This not only enlarges the scope of their operations, but gives elasticity to their capital, and avoids the accumulation of idle balances of money when for any reason their purchases do not keep pace with their sales. Under normal conditions credit is a useful lubricant of industry and commerce.

The circumstances of post-war Europe have given credit a new importance. The scarcity of commodities and the scantiness of production have made the traders of the Continent dependent on supplies from abroad. We have seen how the intensity of their need has itself depressed the value of the paper money in which the liquid portion of their capital is held. The great stock of purchasing power, representing the proceeds of the sales of irreplaceable commodities at apparently extravagant prices during the war, has melted away almost to nothing. They have been confronted with the necessity of *borrowing from abroad*, as the indispensable condition of a resumption of industry and trade. But here too the discredit of the monetary unit has baffled them. How can any foreign financier be expected to lend a sum repayable in a unit the vagaries of which defy calculation? Alternatively how can the borrower, whose transactions in his own country are calculated in this unit, give an undertaking to repay in a foreign currency the exchange value of which may be doubled in a few weeks? Even in the limited class of producers for export, whose receipts will also be in foreign currencies, the difficulty is not removed. The discredited currencies from time to time move upwards as well as downwards, and though hitherto they have taken three steps down for every one step up, a borrower may easily find all his calculations upset by an unexpected rise. German exporters were seriously embarrassed in the summer of 1920 when the exchange value of the mark rose from 1 cent to 3 cents in two or three months. Though the movements of the mark did not affect the relation of the price of the materials bought abroad to that of the finished product, yet the relative enhancement of the other expenses of production was sufficient to turn a profit into a loss. Moreover, those exporters who buy materials in one foreign country and sell their products in another have to take account of three different currencies.

These credit problems, which confront those who are directly concerned in the restoration of trade and industry, have gained more attention than any other aspect of the currency breakdown. They are indeed the most direct result

of the loss of stability of the monetary unit of account.   For
that unit is the unit for the calculation of debts (or credits).
Most of the remedies proposed have taken the form either of
expressing debts, as between people of different countries,
in terms of some other medium than the money of account,
or of supporting debts with a collateral security so expressed.

Various plans have been put forward for creating new
international currencies.   But these would really do nothing.
It is no easier for a trader in one of the distressed countries
to contract to pay in a new currency than in dollars or sterling
or gold.   And such plans are in reality only favoured because
it is tacitly assumed that the issuing authority would generously
create as much of the new currency as traders want.   Needless
to say, this would mean that it in turn would suffer discredit.
Such schemes were wisely negatived by the Brussels Conference of 1920.

The proposal which emerged from that Conference was the
Ter Meulen Scheme.   This scheme is based not on a new
unit for reckoning indebtedness, but on the provision of
collateral security to safeguard an exporter against loss.   It is
a well-thought-out scheme, and avoids many of the pitfalls
with which the problem is beset.   Its weak points would seem
to be : firstly, that it does nothing to make borrowing safe to
the importer, who will in case of difficulty merely have his
Government as creditor instead of the exporter ; secondly, that
the collateral security is to take the form of a State revenue,
the foreclosure of which would merely intensify or revive the
budget difficulties which are causing all the trouble.

The budget again !   This route, like all others, leads back
to the budget.   And we have still to examine the revenue side
of the budget.   The common-sense remedy for a budget deficit
is more taxation.   Perhaps if Europe had grasped this simple
truth two years ago, the worst of the trouble might have been
avoided.   But the breakdown of the currency has itself made
taxation difficult.   The *apparent* revenue has grown, it is true,
beyond all comparison with the nominal pre-war figure.   But
the automatic growth merely records the fall in the value of

6 *

the unit. If the depreciation of the unit be allowed for, the revenue has everywhere become much less productive.

In the case of indirect taxes, which are paid by the mass of the people, the reason is clear. Money wages have been kept down in proportion to the cost of rationed foodstuffs, and the margin left to pay for other commodities is diminished relatively to the high free prices charged for them. Consequently the consumption of the commodities which are suitable vehicles of indirect taxation is reduced. In other words the people are too poor to consume luxuries or to pay taxes. Customs duties produce little when imports are almost confined to necessary supplies acquired by the Government itself.

As has already been explained, the system of enabling the working-class population to subsist on very low money wages, by supplying them with rationed foods at controlled prices, tends to concentrate the surplus income of the community in the hands of those who deal in commodities. The redundant money swells profits, and it is among the profit-earners that the taxable capacity of the country is to be found.

Accordingly the Finance Ministers of Europe have resorted to direct taxation, especially to income taxes and capital levies. But in the administration of these taxes they have encountered an almost insuperable difficulty in the variability of the monetary unit. The assessment of income for taxation cannot begin (at any rate in the case of the profits of trade) till the end of the year of which the income is to be ascertained. It can hardly be completed till some months after the end of the year, and even then some interval must be allowed to the taxpayer to pay. By the time he pays, the assessment is obsolete; it is based on a value of the monetary unit which has become a matter of ancient history. A tax which was intended to be 20 per cent. of his income is perhaps no more than 2 per cent. Nor is this the whole of the evil. The most difficult incomes to assess are the profits of trade. But the collapse of the currency not only makes these incomes much bigger relatively to others, such as house rents, salaries, or interest, but makes them more difficult to assess than ever. When trade conditions are approximately stable, the revenue officials can arrive at some estimate, vague though it be, of the income derived from a business from the outward characteristics of the business and from the style of living of the proprietor.   But, when prices lose all stability, such estimates become valueless.   The tax-payer himself hardly knows his own position; the mere difference between valuing his stock in trade at cost or at replacement value may be enough to transform his balance sheet.

Similar difficulties arise in the administration of a capital levy.   Here, too, a considerable interval must elapse between the assessment and the payment of the tax, and some of the problems of valuation are almost insoluble.   What is intended to be a heroic measure to restore equilibrium once and for all may turn out to be a very modest contribution towards the deficit of one year.

Under normal conditions a budget deficit, which cannot be made good from taxation, can be covered by a loan.   But an internal loan is just the kind of transaction which is made impossible by the instability of the monetary unit.   The Government asks the contributors to surrender large capital sums in return for an annual payment of interest, and possibly an ultimate repayment of the capital.   But can the Government undertake to make these future payments in a unit which may have appreciated to several times its present value?   Or can the contributors accept its promises to pay, when the unit may on the contrary depreciate till it is almost worthless?   The bargain is a gamble which may turn out to be disastrous to either party.   And in any case it is difficult to induce people to put their money into gilt-edged securities, when inflation with its swollen trading profits is in full swing.   A forced loan would avoid a part of these objections, but not that on the score of the possible increase of the burden of repayment should the currency unit appreciate.   And it raises the same difficulties as a tax, since the contributions must be determined by assessments upon the contributors' capital or income.

If all possible efforts, both for restraining expenditure and raising revenue, still leave a deficit uncovered, and if the necessary sum cannot be borrowed at home, there remains the possibility of borrowing abroad. To the harassed finance minister, a foreign loan appears as a happy dream. In it he sees a *deus ex machina*, who will cure all his troubles. The loan will just give that breathing-space in which production and business can recover; if it rather more than covers the immediate deficit, a portion can be used as a reserve for stabilising the currency; and there is a reasonable chance that, when it is exhausted, the productivity of the ordinary sources of revenue will have been restored. These advantages are real, and it is probable that two years ago, if the financially stronger countries had been prepared, at some sacrifice and risk to themselves, to lend more liberally to their distressed neighbours, the extremity of the present catastrophe might have been avoided. But many circumstances combined to prevent this. For one thing, the most distressed countries of all had been on the defeated side in the war, and public opinion among the victors was hardly prepared to entertain proposals for giving them pecuniary aid. Indeed the victorious powers were hoping themselves to extract money from them to meet their own budget deficits. Demobilisation was slow, and the expense of winding up war commitments was gigantic. To transfer to their shoulders part of the burden of Eastern Europe might have irretrievably destroyed their own financial equilibrium. They were themselves suffering from the evils of inflation. This was obvious enough in the case of France, England, and Italy where a premium on gold already existed and steadily increased from March, 1919, when freedom was restored to the foreign exchanges. But it was true even of the United States. The exchanges in New York on England France, and Italy had only been fixed at the cost of allowing the exchanges on many neutral countries to rise to a premium during the war. It was for some time in doubt whether the dollar could be maintained at its gold par, and the export of gold from the United States continued to be prohibited till 9th June, 1919. Nor did the gold standard itself prevent inflation from occurring. The demand for gold as currency was confined to the United States, Spain, Argentina, Uruguay, and Japan. The loss of gold by export within so limited a field was insufficient to operate as a check upon credit expansion, and such an expansion occurred on a great scale in the twelve months ending with June, 1920.   An even greater expansion occurred at the same time in England, where the gold standard was not effective.   In both countries the expansion was mainly due to trade borrowing, and differed therein from the inflation which was brought about on the Continent by excessive issues of paper money.   But, for all that, it had the same effect of making business so profitable that no money could be spared from trade for investment in Government securities.   This was the real reason why the great investment markets were closed at the critical time to borrowers from distressed Europe.

The fact that the credit expansion has now given place to an equally violent contraction is therefore not without its compensations.   At a time of trade depression, unpleasant though it is, there is a tendency to transfer money from trade to investment, especially in gilt-edged securities.   For some of the distressed countries the opportunity may come too late. Their economic power may be so radically impaired that investors will not entrust money to them.   But those which can hold out a reasonable prospect of full recuperation, or in other words of a solvent budget and a stable currency, will no longer be precluded from borrowing by scarcity of investible funds.   This does not mean that advances will be made by one Government to another.   It means that the private investor will be willing to lend money in relatively liberal amounts and at rates of interest which, even if high according to pre-war ideas, will be moderate in comparison with those which have recently been exacted.

How is a country to proceed when the change makes itself felt and aid is at last offered ?   Its financial programme is a matter of vital importance, for the investors themselves will not come forward unless they are convinced that the way to solvency is open.   It is easy to say that the currency must be stabilised, but the brief examination that we have made of monetary conditions in Eastern Europe shows only too clearly how perplexing that problem is.   If the proceeds of the foreign loan are simply used to cover the deficit and to pay for the Government's purchases abroad, the issue of paper money can be stopped. That would be an immense gain. But it would not by itself secure confidence in the monetary unit. Though there would be less reason to fear an indefinite depreciation of its value, it would still be impossible to say what its true value ought to be within very wide limits. That power of calculating upon the future which is so essential to credit transactions would still be absent.

What is wanted is a definite decision as to the future value of the unit in relation to other currencies. Unfortunately pounds, francs, and dollars vary in relation to one another, but if the unit can be fixed in relation to one sound foreign currency that will be enough to give confidence. This can be effected by what is known as an exchange standard. Funds are obtained in the foreign country whose currency has been selected as a standard, and the Government (or a bank acting on behalf of the Government) undertakes to buy and sell credits in that country in exchange for its own currency in unlimited quantities at a fixed rate of exchange.

But, it may be asked, are the precious foreign credits to be dissipated in buying up valueless paper money? By no means. That is not the real significance of the transaction. As a result of inflation, the country has been left bare of commodities, and full of paper money. To fix the value of the monetary unit is to give the holders of that paper money the power to acquire commodities in exchange for it. By doing so the people secure the most urgently needed foreign supplies just as effectively as if the Government spent the proceeds of the foreign loan on buying them. And at the same time forward transactions in the monetary unit become possible, so that traders can borrow on their own account through private channels in order to obtain materials. Trade and production, and with them the taxable capacity of the country, can be restored in this way, or, if not, they cannot be restored at all.

Success depends upon a judicious choice of the new exchange value of the monetary unit. This is not an easy

matter to settle, when different tests of the existing depreciation give, as we have seen, widely divergent results. The
most obvious value to choose is the actual market rate of
exchange. But if, as is probable, this exhibits a greater
degree of depreciation than any other test (except prices
directly dependent on it), that means that a very large
adjustment has to be made in wages and prices. And, to
avoid this, it may be advisable to raise the value of the unit
somewhat above that ruling in the exchange market.

It is essential that the working-classes should be able to
live on their wages. Either the prices of necessaries, including
those supplied from abroad, must be brought down to the
proper proportion to wages, or wages must be raised to the
proper proportion to prices. The fall in the prices of foreign
commodities comes automatically with an improvement of the
exchange ; whereas, if prices are fixed at a high level, it may
take a long time for wages to be adapted.

Further, if the value of the monetary unit is fixed very
low, the capital of those traders who have parted with most of
their stock in trade, and hold the proceeds in paper money or
bank credits, may be so restricted as to interfere seriously
with a resumption of business.

On the other hand, the higher the value of the unit the
greater the reserve of foreign currency needed. For a large
reserve will certainly be required in proportion to the stock
of paper money in circulation. The opportunity of spending
this paper money in foreign markets must be a reality, and
multitudes of people with large accumulations of paper money
will rush to take advantage of it. Much of the reserve will
melt away ; if it is exhausted, and the exchangeability of the
currency into foreign credits is suspended, confidence will be
at an end. Once the first rush is over, the reserve may be
expected to grow again. People are willing to hold larger
balances of a currency which they trust, and, budget embarrassments being supposed past, they can only procure currency
in exchange for foreign credits, which will go to swell the
reserve, and which may raise it even above its original amount.
For in the countries we are considering the stock of currency

in circulation, if reckoned at its existing exchange value, is remarkably low. Even with a substantially higher exchange value, it would still be inadequate for the needs of the community, were business restored to a normal state of activity. The revived absorption of currency should contribute most valuable additional resources for the process of reconstruction.

It must not be assumed that the restoration of credit cannot be achieved without a foreign loan. Helpful though a foreign loan would be in all cases of currency difficulty, it is not essential, unless the evil has gone so far that the productive machine has itself become paralysed.

There are some countries in Eastern Europe which, despite such a depreciation of the monetary unit as before the war would have been thought insupportable, are nevertheless steadily returning towards normal productivity. If by severe taxation and drastic economy in public expenditure they can balance their budgets, then they can avoid fresh issues of paper money, and can eventually stabilise their currency. Stabilisation, however, is much more difficult without a foreign loan, not merely because a greater immediate burden has to be placed upon the taxpayer, but because it is necessary to start regulating the currency before it is possible to prescribe any definite standard of value. The standard has to be evolved by experience. One of the first measures must be the abandonment of control over prices, wages, and the foreign exchanges. The market must settle the value of the monetary unit, and for this purpose it must be *free*. Only so will values of goods and services acquire their proper relative proportions, and, until they do, the value of the unit has no definite significance. Moreover, we have already seen how the anomalies in relative values which spring from price controls militate against efficient taxation, and how the controls themselves swell the public expenditure and discourage production. The abolition of such controls would seem to be the most fruitful first step that can be taken.

But it would be a grave error to disregard the dangers which attend this first step. There might follow a period of extreme instability of prices, markets having no clear guidance in estimating the future value of the monetary unit. The danger would be reduced to a minimum if the controlled prices could be raised, before control ceases, approximately to what their free level is likely to be. This would necessitate a preliminary settlement, even if only a provisional one, of what the value of the unit is to be, and would place on the Government, the delicate task of estimating the future free prices. The same perplexities arise as in the case where a foreign loan is obtained. If the value of the monetary unit is fixed low, then large adjustments in prices and wages are necessary. If the value of the unit is fixed high, there is much more danger that the existing issue of paper money will be found to be redundant, and a new cycle of rising prices and loss of confidence be started.

If the first step be supposed successfully taken, and free prices established in the markets, the next measure is to refuse to issue any more paper money except in exchange for foreign credits at a fixed rate of exchange. The effectiveness of this proceeding depends on there being an unsatisfied demand for legal tender money. The first return to free markets may be supposed to have found trade at a low ebb; the revival of business should create the necessary demand for currency. But if the country is suffering from scarcity there is some risk that the rush to buy supplies from abroad may not have exhausted itself, and may occasion a redundancy, before any new demand for currency has materialised. The Government, having no reserve against its paper circulation, cannot undertake to sell exchange (i.e. redeem paper money) at a fixed rate.

The stability of the currency may also be imperilled by an *appreciation* of the foreign monetary unit by reference to which it is regulated. In the latter half of 1920 there was a very great appreciation of the purchasing power of the American dollar in relation both to commodities and to the currencies of other countries. The appreciation of the pound sterling was nearly as great. Other currencies, which remained stable in relation to commodities, became redundant and depreciated *relatively* to the pound and dollar.

The conspicuous strengthening of the credit position in America should lead to a relaxation of the severe regime of deflation which has been in operation there since the spring of 1920, and should bring about a reaction in the dollar. This particular difficulty will then for the time being be removed.

V.

THE FEDERAL RESERVE SYSTEM OF THE UNITED STATES.[1]

A COMBINATION of circumstances gives the banking system of the United States a special interest for us at the present time. Not only is the theoretical study of the working of the Federal Reserve Act, which was one of the most comprehensive measures of banking reform ever carried, facilitated by the wealth of statistics available, but American economic conditions have acquired a far greater importance in the world than before the war, and in particular, in that the dollar has been kept on a gold basis, the Americans are in a position to affect very materially the prospects of currency reform in the Old World.

It is not possible to understand the Federal Reserve Act without some reference to the pre-existing banking system, and of this I must therefore interpose a very brief explanation. Among all the complexities of American banking, regulated, as it is, concurrently by Federal and State legislation, one or two salient principles emerge. In the first place, with unimportant exceptions, American banks are prohibited from having branches. The result is an amazing multiplication of banks, large and small, the total number in 1914 being 24,668 (exclusive of 2100 savings banks). One consequence is that clearing operations are far more complicated than in a system of big banks with branches. A hierarchy of clearing centres is necessary. The banks in the smaller centres act as clearing agents for the neighbouring country banks, and in turn keep accounts with banks in the larger centres, which act as their agents. In some respects, though not in all, the relation of a

---

[1] Read before the Royal Statistical Society, 21st February, 1922.

bank to its clearing agent reproduces that of a branch to its head office. In the United States, before the passage of the Federal Reserve Act, the clearing organisations, and especially that of New York, which was the apex of all, had come to play a very prominent part. In any group of banks the signal that one of the group has been too liberal in granting credit is an excessive balance against it at the clearing house. In times of crisis, when all banks were running short of cash, it had become the practice temporarily to relieve banks from meeting such balances in cash, provided they deposited adequate security with the clearing house. In return for that security they received "clearing house certificates," with which they were allowed to pay the balances due. This process was a rudimentary analogue of the rediscounting facilities given by the great European Central banks. It was an expedient born of sheer necessity, and was itself evidence of the urgent need for reform.

One of the most characteristic features of the American banking system is the statutory reserve proportion. In the case of the national banks (that is to say, those with charters under Federal law, which alone are privileged to be banks of issue) this proportion depends upon the locality in which the bank is. New York, Chicago, and St. Louis are central reserve cities. About fifty other towns (required to be of not less than 50,000 inhabitants) are classed as reserve cities. In the reserve and central reserve cities, before the change made by the Federal Reserve Act, every national bank had always to retain a cash reserve equal to 25 per cent. of its deposits; elsewhere the prescribed proportion was 15 per cent. But of this 15 per cent. three-fifths could be held in the form of deposits in national banks in the reserve or central reserve cities, while national banks in the reserve cities were allowed to keep half their 25 per cent. reserves in the form of deposits in the central reserve cities. In these last the whole 25 per cent. reserves had to be held in lawful money. Thus, in reality, the country banks had only to keep 6 per cent. of their deposits in actual cash, and banks in reserve cities 12½ per cent. This arrangement, by which deposits could be counted as reserves, was designed to fit in with the clearing arrangements. It was recognised that a credit with a clearing agent might be as important to a non-central bank as actual cash.

The banks incorporated under State laws are not subject to the National Bank Act. But the State laws, though often less stringent than the federal, do not differ fundamentally from them, and, apart from the fact that they are precluded (not by an express prohibition, but by a prohibitive federal tax) from issuing bank notes, the State banks and the "trust companies" (which are only banks under another name) differ little in type from the national banks.

The Federal Reserve Act may be described as a measure for introducing the rediscounting central bank system. It sets up not one but twelve separate banks, but each is "central" in that it is alone in its own district, and all are subject to a co-ordinating body, the Federal Reserve Board, whose powers are sufficient to impose something like unity of policy on the whole. All national banks *must*, and State banks and trust companies with the requisite capital *may*, enter the system and become "member banks." By doing so the latter put themselves to that extent under federal banking law, and the old distinction between them and the national banks has become blurred. The capital of the Federal Reserve Banks is wholly subscribed by the member banks themselves, each subscribing an amount equal to 6 per cent. of its own capital.

Every member bank has the right of having "eligible paper" rediscounted by the Federal Reserve Bank of its district. Eligible paper includes notes or bills drawn "for agricultural, industrial, or commercial purposes," but not those "covering merely investments or issued or drawn for the purpose of carrying or trading in stocks, bonds, or other investment securities, except bonds and notes of the Government of the United States." Apart from the last-named ominous exception, the test of the eligibility of the paper is the surplus of "quick assets" possessed by the borrower who originally raised money on it. In America the banking accommodation given to internal trade takes the form neither of bills of exchange, such as are customary in Europe, nor of simple advances, such as we have in this country, but of promissory notes. These notes, while depending like a bank advance on the sole credit of the borrower, unsupported by any other name, resemble a bill, in that they can be rediscounted. And though efforts are being made to introduce bills of exchange, single-name notes still form far the greater part of the paper dealt with by the American banks. A large proportion, perhaps the majority, of the notes are eligible for rediscount, and the right of rediscount has made the position of the ordinary American bank far more liquid than before. This improved liquidity was regarded as a justification for a relaxation of the reserve provisions. In the Federal Reserve Act, as originally passed, the proportions were fixed at 18 per cent. instead of 25 in central reserve cities, 15 instead of 25 in reserve cities, and 12 instead of 15 elsewhere. But only *one-third* of the reserve in each case had to be in cash, and the remainder could be (and a prescribed portion had to be) on deposit in the Federal Reserve Bank. On the other hand, no portion of the reserve could (after the lapse of a preliminary interval) be held in any other bank. These provisions were entirely recast by an amending Act of 22nd June, 1917, soon after the entry of the United States into the war. Under this Act the *whole* reserve has to be on deposit with the Federal Reserve Bank, the cash held by any member bank being left to its unfettered discretion, and the proportions are reduced to 13, 10, and 7 per cent.[1]

Thus, the statutory reserves have ceased altogether to be cash, and are now solely credit. When they fall below the prescribed proportion, they can be replenished by rediscounting eligible paper. Formerly the occurrence of a general shortage of cash led to a convulsive contraction of credit by all the banks, and in extreme cases to a general suspension of cash payments. A national bank, of which the reserve falls below

---

[1] These proportions apply only to demand deposits. For time deposits the proportion was originally 5 per cent. and was reduced by the Act of June, 1917, to 3 per cent. for all localities.

the statutory proportion, is forbidden to make any new loans till the proportion is restored.   When reserves meant cash, and there was no machinery for making good a general shortage of cash, the result of such a shortage was a general refusal to lend, which was only too likely to precipitate a crisis.   Now, on the contrary, the material from which reserves are manufactured is eligible paper, and, so long as the supply of that is adequate, this *impasse* will not occur.   Moreover, the Federal Reserve Board is given discretion to suspend any reserve requirement (subject to a graduated tax on the deficiency), so that even if a member bank's supply of eligible paper runs out, it can still be enabled to continue to accommodate its customers.

This elasticity of reserves has removed one of the gravest faults in the old national banking system, and one to which much of the virulence of past American crises has been due.

The substitution of reserves deposited with the Federal Reserve banks for reserves held partly in cash and partly on deposit with other national banks, has been logically accompanied by a reform in the clearing system.   An endeavour has been made, with a considerable measure of success, to concentrate the clearings in the Federal Reserve banks which, it may be mentioned, have a number of branches.   Subordinate centres still exist, and the less central national banks still carry balances in the more central.   But these balances no longer count as reserves, and as all member banks in any case have balances with the Federal Reserve banks, the old hierarchy of clearing centres has lost some of its importance.   And the Federal Reserve banks have established a system of clearing cheques from all over the country, as nearly as possible free of charge, even for non-member banks which choose to participate in it.

One of the purposes of the Federal Reserve Act is expressly stated in its title to be "to furnish an elastic currency."   This is a function which is intimately related to that of rediscounting.   A balance with a central bank can, of course, always be drawn out in legal tender money.   The same rediscounting system which enables member banks to replenish their balances

7

with the Federal Reserve banks equally enables them to draw out currency. To meet such demands the Federal Reserve banks are given certain powers of issue. They issue two different kinds of notes, Federal Reserve notes and Federal Reserve *bank notes*. The latter are of quite secondary importance; they are merely intended to replace gradually the national bank notes, the notes issued by the national banks against United States Government Bonds.[1]

The important new issue is that of Federal Reserve notes. Federal Reserve notes are ultimately obligations of the United States Government, but they are issued through a Federal Reserve bank, and they become liabilities of the issuing bank. They are not legal tender, but are convertible into lawful money[2] on presentation at the issuing bank, or into gold on presentation at the Treasury in Washington. They are issued to Federal Reserve banks in exchange either for " eligible paper " or for gold. Eligible paper and gold are, of course, the principal assets of the Federal Reserve banks, which are thus enabled to meet any demands which could possibly be made upon them for currency, provided (as may safely be assumed) that the Federal Reserve notes, though not legal tender, are as freely accepted as any other medium of payment.

The Federal Reserve banks are thus fully equipped to supply their member banks both with the credits which constitute their statutory reserves and clearing-house balances, and also with currency to meet the demands of circulation. To ensure the maintenance of the gold standard, they are required to keep reserves against their liabilities. Against their deposits they must keep at least 35 per cent. in lawful money; against

---

[1] Only certain classes of bonds can be used for this purpose, and as the supply of them is limited, the note-issue is correspondingly limited. The bonds, with the right of issue, are gradually to be surrendered by the national banks to the Federal Reserve banks, which will thus acquire the right to issue Federal Reserve bank notes. A special additional issue of Federal Reserve bank notes has been made under the Pittman Act of 1918 to take the place of the silver certificates withdrawn in consequence of the sale of silver under that Act in India.

[2] " Lawful money " includes, besides gold, gold certificates, standard dollars, silver certificates and United States notes (greenbacks), but all these latter are convertible into gold.

the Federal Reserve notes they issue they must keep at least 40 per cent. in gold. These reserve requirements, like all others, can be suspended, subject to the payment of a graduated tax, by the Federal Reserve Board.[1]

These, then, are the salient provisions of this great banking reform. From 16th November, 1914, when the Act was inaugurated, till the entry of the United States into the war in 1917, the Federal Reserve banks played quite a secondary part in American banking. The reason was twofold. In the first place, the State banks were unwilling to join the system; and secondly, owing to the large inflow of gold from Europe, there was very little need for rediscounting. In March, 1917, when the deposits in the Federal Reserve banks and the Federal Reserve notes in circulation together exceeded $1000 millions, rediscounts amounted to only $20 millions. The gold reserves amounted to no less than $938 millions. The Federal Reserve Banks could not really gain control till the need for rediscounts was felt.

It was the outbreak of war that made the system effective. First of all war finance placed upon the United States the tremendous burden of financing not only her own belligerent requirements, but the voracious needs of her allies. This meant inflation. The sums were too vast to be obtained exclusively from investible savings, and recourse was had to the banks.[2] Inflation soon stopped the influx of gold, and threatened an efflux. In September, 1917, the export of gold was prohibited. As the deposit liabilities of the banks grew, they were compelled to make up their reserve proportions by rediscounting. Meanwhile the amending Act of 22nd June, 1917, had required the *whole* of the statutory reserves (though reduced) to be on deposit with the Federal Reserve banks. The effect is seen in the growth of the deposits from $721 millions in May to $1262 millions in June. The same Act

---

[1] For the reserve against Federal Reserve notes the graduated tax is expressly required not to be less than certain prescribed rates.

[2] From Table III it will be seen that the total investments of all the banks in the United States rose from $4663 millions in June, 1916, to $9441 millions in June, 1919. In March they are estimated to have reached $10,000 millions.

facilitated the entry of State banks into the system, especially (1) by securing them the continuance as far as possible of the rights they enjoyed under their State charters, and (2) by enabling them to leave the system again on reasonable notice, should they desire to do so. The State bank and trust company membership, which included in June, 1917, only 3·56 per cent. of all the capital of such banks, had grown in June, 1918, to 23·82 per cent., and in June, 1919, to 29·62 per cent. (see Table II, p. 125).

Inflation also led to a rising demand for currency, which could only be supplied by the issue of Federal Reserve notes against eligible paper, that is to say, by rediscounting. But this demand for currency was at first more than met by the cash released through the alteration in the reserve laws. The cash held by all the banks of the United States (other than Federal Reserve banks) fell from $1442 millions in June, 1917, to $839 millions in June, 1918. In the same period the total money in circulation in the country outside the Federal Reserve banks, but including that in the other banks, rose from $4153 millions to $4283 millions. The apparently small increase of $130 millions conceals a real increase exceeding $700 millions in the hands of the public outside the banks. By the time of the armistice the cash in circulation had risen to $5000 millions, of which about $1000 millions was in the banks. The Federal Reserve notes in circulation were growing steadily all the time, from $463 millions on 1st June, 1917, to $1577 millions on 1st June, 1918, and $2532 millions on 1st November, 1918. Thus, by the time of the armistice half the currency in active circulation consisted of Federal Reserve notes. The combined effect of inflation and increased membership of the Federal Reserve system is seen in the rise of deposits in the Federal Reserve banks to $1663 millions.

Up to this point the practical operation of the Federal Reserve system had been on the whole simply to facilitate inflation. Expansible reserve deposits and an expansible currency had enabled the banks to continue that augmentation of purchasing power which had depended till 1917 on the steady influx of gold from Europe. In November, 1918, the Federal Reserve banks held a total cash reserve of $2105 millions, the statutory reserves (35 per cent. of deposits, *plus* 40 per cent. of notes) came to $1588 millions, and therefore they had a surplus reserve of $517 millions. With so substantial a margin had they come through the period of war inflation.

In the months following the armistice no step was taken to contract credit. The reserve position being what it was, no such step seemed necessary. Nevertheless, the cessation of war conditions brought about spontaneously a pause in the inflationary process. Prices of commodities reacted a little, the expansion in bank deposits stopped, currency circulation fell. But the pause did not last long. By May the prices of commodities had recovered and (as measured by the Bureau of Labour index number) were as high as at any time during the war. May was the month in which the big "Victory Loan" was subscribed, and about that time the banks' holdings of United States Government securities touched a maximum. The quarter ended 30th September, 1919, was the last in which expenditure exceeded revenue. The pegging of the foreign exchanges had just ceased. The prohibition on the export of gold was removed on 7th June. By 30th June, 1919, the day of the usual annual returns from all the banks of the United States, the hesitancy which followed the armistice was over. Credit expansion was definitely restarted. In Table III (p. 126) will be found estimates of the deposits, loans, investments, and cash of all the banks in the United States for a number of dates between 30th June, 1918, and 30th June, 1921. The figures are calculated from the returns of member banks of the Federal Reserve system. From 1st November, 1918, to 4th March, 1919, deposits were practically stationary; investments increased from $8759 millions to $10,082 millions; loans and discounts fell from $19,974 to $19,359 millions. The short interval from March to June saw both deposits and loans and discounts jump up by about $2000 millions.

Unlike those of the preceding two years, this was a credit

expansion arising from purely commercial causes, and not from the expedients of Government finance. Credit was expanded by the banks in response to trade demands. This situation raised the question of the responsibility of the Federal Reserve Board for controlling credit. The new system was on its trial. It had been put forward as a remedy for financial crisis. Panic had come time after time in the past as the catastrophic termination of a period of credit expansion. The immediate occasion for it had then been the depletion of cash reserves. The Federal Reserve system was planned to meet this danger by giving almost unlimited re-discounting facilities, as well as a discretion to suspend reserve requirements temporarily. To the practical banker approaching the problems of credit from the point of view of one institution among 30,000, these powers solved the problem. But the same forces which had depleted cash reserves in 1907, in 1893 or in 1873, remained ever ready to operate. Credit expansion would still lead to an increased internal demand for currency and to an export of gold. And the Federal Reserve system took account of this part of the problem of credit control in that it prescribed the reserve proportions for notes and deposits. If the Federal Reserve Board, conscious of its duty not merely to help every individual bank, but to deal with the credit situation as a whole, asked for guidance, here was the answer. The signal for a contraction of credit was to be the fall of the reserve proportions towards the limit.

At the last return in June, 1919, the reserve position of the Federal Reserve Banks was a little stronger than at the armistice, the surplus being $604 millions. The amount was ample. The signal for contraction had not been given. Six months later the situation had changed profoundly. At the end of December the surplus reserve had fallen to $315 millions. This was due partly to a drop of $80 millions in cash reserves, but mainly to an increase of $558 millions in the circulation of Federal Reserve notes. The money actually in the hands of the public had increased by $470 millions, so that $88 millions had been needed to replace other money lost from circulation. In fact, there had been net exports of gold to the amount of no less than $187 millions.[1]

Few as the remaining gold standard countries were, their demands were still important enough to occasion a drain of gold exceeding all precedent.

In November the Federal Reserve Board had taken a first practical step towards controlling credit. In order to facilitate the absorption of Government securities the rate of discount on paper secured by them had till then been fixed low (usually 4 or $4\frac{1}{4}$ per cent., as compared with $4\frac{1}{2}$ or $4\frac{3}{4}$ in most other cases). Far the greater part of the rediscounts were at these preferential rates, and in fact the average rate for all rediscount transactions by the Federal Reserve banks in October, 1919, was 4·19 per cent. Early in November this preference was discontinued, and the rate was put up to $4\frac{1}{2}$ per cent., the average for November being 4·54 per cent. Some further slight rises in December brought the average to 4·67.

Meanwhile the Federal Reserve Board, being fully aware of the inflationary tendencies at work, repeatedly exhorted the banking community to be cautious in lending, and in particular to refuse accommodation for speculation or for transactions in non-essential commodities.

Neither exhortation nor the rise in the rediscount rate had any visible effects. The decline in the reserve position at the end of December, however, was not in itself a decisive sign. A drain of cash into circulation during the autumn months and up to the end of the year is usual, and an abnormal loss of gold in the period following the removal of the export prohibition was to be expected. But with the new year there was no recovery. After some oscillations, the surplus reserve on January 23 was still only $314 millions, and it was decided to take more drastic action. The rediscount rate was put up to $5\frac{1}{2}$ per cent. on paper secured by United States bonds, and to 6 per cent. for ordinary commercial paper; only paper

[1] The recorded net exports were $321 millions, but gold to the amount of $134 millions received in respect of relief to Germany and deposited in London to the credit of the New York Federal Reserve Bank, has to be counted as an "import," though it was not actually imported till late in 1920. But it counted towards the reserve as soon as it was deposited.

secured by Treasury "Certificates of Indebtedness" (the American equivalent of our Treasury Bills) retained for a time the preferential rate of $4\frac{3}{4}$ per cent. This meant a predominant rate of $5\frac{1}{2}$ per cent., and 6 per cent. for any member bank which might exhaust its stock of paper secured by Government securities.

The market rates of discount for commercial paper quickly responded. From $5\frac{1}{4}$ per cent. in October the rate (in New York) rose to $5\frac{1}{2}$ per cent. at the end of November, and 6 per cent. in December. Early in February it rose fractionally above 6 per cent., and by the end of February it was almost 7 per cent.[1]

The successive rises in the rediscount rate were not made without some searchings of heart. The Federal Reserve Board had several times expressed a certain scepticism as to the effectiveness of the rediscount rate in checking credit expansion. The Bank of England had successfully controlled credit in the past by means of the bank rate, but London was a great centre of international trade. Moreover, the margin of profit to which dealers were accustomed in America was supposed to be larger than in England, and American business would be correspondingly less sensitive to the rediscount rate.

But exhortation had no noticeable effect on the banks,

---

[1] It is sometimes argued that the rediscount rate ought to be a *maximum*, and that, when the market rate is above it, that is a sign that the rediscount rate is not effective. The argument proceeds from a fallacious comparison with the London market. The London counterpart of the ordinary "commercial paper" of New York, the one-name promissory note, is not the bill of exchange, but the bank advance. Bank advances, not being embodied in any negotiable document, cannot be rediscounted at all, and they are usually made at a fixed rate of say 1 per cent. above bank rate. Bills are discounted at a low rate because they are readily saleable in the market, and are almost the equivalent of cash. The bank rate, though usually above the market rate of discount, is below the prevailing rate of interest on advances. In London rediscounts are only an occasional phenomena, and are usually small in amount.

In New York, and in all the Federal Reserve districts, a large volume of rediscounts is always outstanding. Unless there is a margin between the rates of discount and rediscount, a rediscount absorbs the whole profit of the member bank upon the note in question. As soon as the rediscount rate is raised, it begins to push up the discount rate till the margin is sufficient to give adequate compensation to the member banks. Apparently about 1 per cent. is what they regard as a suitable margin.

and, if the first tentative increases in the rate of rediscount in
November were equally ineffective, the fault might be that
they did not go far enough. Whatever the faults of the rediscount rate might be as an instrument for controlling credit,
the Federal Reserve Board were faced with the fact that *they
had no other*.

In one respect the rise to 6 per cent. in January seemed
to have a very real effect. Ever since the early months of
1919 American traders had been exporting on an enormous
scale to Europe. The European purchasers paid in their own
currencies, which had been left, since the unpegging of the
exchanges in 1919, to find their level. Deprived of artificial
support and exposed to the full effects of the desperate inflation
which had characterised European war finance, the value of
these currency units in the exchange market fell steadily. The
American exporters did not at first appreciate what was happening. Misled, perhaps, by the "balance of trade" fallacy,
they regarded the depreciation of the European currencies
as a temporary phenomenon, and they decided to leave the
balances lying to their credit, till a return to normal conditions
might enable them to remit them to America without loss.
To hold these balances, it was necessary in many cases for the
exporters to receive advances in dollars from their bankers.
But by the end of 1919 the depreciation in some cases had
reached such a pitch that the prospect of a recovery was
becoming remote, whatever happened to the balance of trade.
Sterling was no more than 23 per cent. below par; but French
and Belgian francs were depreciated 60 per cent. ; Italian lire
70 per cent. ; German marks and the debris of the Austro-
Hungarian crowns were reduced to mere fractions of their
par values. Not only was the wisdom of waiting becoming
doubtful, but these shrinking balances of paper money were
beginning to afford inadequate security for the advances made
to their possessors. At the end of January the banks suddenly
began to call in their loans, and the exchange market was
struck with something approaching to panic. Even sterling
fell to $3·20, raising the extent of its depreciation to 34 per
cent. Francs and lire declined rapidly, and the currencies of

Eastern Europe fell in February to about half the value they had commanded in December. The temporary character of the movement is demonstrated by the fact that in a few months these currencies all recovered (with one or two unimportant exceptions) to levels above the December quotations. How far this action on the part of the American banks was occasioned or suggested by the rise in the rediscount rate it is impossible to say. At any rate it is noteworthy as being the first symptom of interruption of the credit expansion which had been gaining momentum since the previous spring.

But in other respects the rise in the discount rate seemed to have little if any effect. The note-issue, which had fallen from $3057 millions, the seasonal maximum touched at the end of December, to $2844 millions on January 23, began to rise steadily, and by the end of February was back at $3000 millions. The gold exports continued. Those to Spain, which in 1919 had amounted to $29·8 millions, had ceased, but those to Argentina and the East were continuing on a large scale. On February 20 the cash reserves of the Federal Reserve banks had fallen to $2035 millions, being $100 millions below the amount on December 31, and the surplus reserve was only $220 millions. The New York Bank actually had a reserve deficiency of $8 millions. At this stage the Treasury deposited $50 millions of silver dollars in the New York Bank with a view to subsequent transmission to the East. But even with this assistance the surplus reserve continued to fall.

Early in March came news that gold was being sent from England. In the course of March and April it arrived to the amount of $56 millions, and in May there followed $23·6 millions on British account from Hong Kong. And at the same time the export of gold began to die down. Argentina took in April nearly $30 millions, making $90 millions since January 1, and $146 millions since the removal of the prohibition on export in June, 1919, but apparently that was enough to reach saturation point. Exports of gold to all quarters in May were only $8 millions. The cash reserves recovered from $2054 millions on 5th March, to $2087 millions on 9th April.   But the note-issue was growing, and the surplus reserve was soon lower than ever.

There were several danger points in view.   In the first place, the gold received from England was in the nature of a windfall.   It might not be repeated, and in any case could not continue indefinitely.   Secondly, though gold exports to South America had stopped, a financial crisis had just broken out in Japan.   The Japanese exchange jumped up to the gold point, and there was every likelihood of large exports of gold thither.   Thirdly, it would soon be necessary to deal with the usual credit strain incidental to the movement of the crops. In 1919 the Federal Reserve note-issue had risen by $550 millions between 1st August and the end of the year.

And by this time the Federal Reserve Board were fully alive to the fact that the reserve position did not tell the whole story.   An expansion of credit and therefore of purchasing power stimulates sales, depletes stocks of commodities, increases orders to producers, raises prices, and altogether makes business at every stage more active and more profitable. Thereby the demand for bank credit is itself again intensified, and a vicious circle of inflation is set up.   In the period we are now considering this process had been working with unprecedented potency, and its effects were clearly to be seen in the prices of commodities.   The Bureau of Labour's index number of prices (the base of which is 100 in 1913) stood at 206 at the end of 1918.[1]   At first it fell, but from a minimum of 197 in February, 1919, it rose to 248 in January, 1920. There was then a pause, but in March the index rose to 253 and in April it jumped to 265.

When credit expansion with the concomitant upward tendency of prices has once set in, a rate of discount, which under normal conditions would be adequate or even high, becomes low relatively to the profits to be derived from the use of borrowed money.   What is needed to secure control is such a rise in the rate as will deter traders from borrowing.

---

[1] Since this was written the Bureau of Labour's index numbers have been revised from the beginning.   But the difference between the revised figures and those here used is not great and is nowhere material to the argument.

But if prices are rising, the mere holding of commodities in stock yields an additional profit over and above the usual dealer's percentage on the turn-over. If traders are to be deterred from borrowing money to buy commodities, the rate of discount must be high enough to offset the additional profit.

But, it may be asked, how is this possible when prices are rising at the rate of 30 per cent. per annum? No one would contemplate a rate of discount of anything approaching such a figure.[1] Yet how can a lower rate be deterrent?

The explanation is that it is not the *past* rise in prices but the *future* rise that has to be counteracted. The problem is a psychological one. As soon as the rate is high enough to offset the traders' hopes of future profits it becomes deterrent. And a very relevant factor in the psychological problem is the traders' expectations as to the intentions of the authority which fixes rates. If that authority means business, and can be relied on to push up rates relentlessly till they become deterrent, the *mere expectation* that this will happen may make quite a moderate rate adequate. For the prospect of rising prices is dispelled and normal standards of profit and interest are re-established in the traders' minds.

In May, 1920, it had become certain that the rediscount rates fixed in January and the corresponding market rates on commercial paper (then fully 7 per cent.) were not adequately deterrent. It was announced that as from 1st June the rediscount rate in New York and Chicago on commercial paper was to be 7 per cent., or, if secured by Liberty Bonds or Victory Notes, 6 per cent. The rate on commercial paper was quickly adjusted to a $7\frac{3}{4}$ per cent. and soon to an 8 per cent. basis.

This was the turning point. The dreaded gold exports to Japan began in July, and before the end of the year had exceeded $90 millions.[2] The expansion in the note issue

---

[1] It is true that the rate of interest on call money in New York occasionally rises to a very high figure, but that is only for a short time. Rates of 20 or 30 per cent. for several months would be quite a different matter.

[2] The very large gold imports from England, $215 millions in the second half of 1920, were swollen by the sending to America of the German gold, till then ear-

continued, and by 24th December it was $300 millions above the total at the end of May. The surplus reserve fell on more than one occasion almost to the low level of May. Nevertheless, the Federal Reserve Board were conscious that they had gained control. The speculative fever had abated.

The maximum price index was recorded in May at 272. The fall, slight at first, gathered way. By November the reduction in some of the most important commodities (especially grain crops and textile materials) was so severe that dealers and producers, together with the banks that financed them, were gravely embarrassed. The price index for that month was 207 and for December 189.[1]

And now, indeed, was the value of the Federal Reserve system felt. With the old banking system nothing could have averted a crash. Everything depended upon the banks throughout the country being able to allow time to borrowers whose expectations of selling at a remunerative price had been disappointed. The frozen credits had to be liquidated. The member banks of the Federal Reserve system were able to maintain their reserve position, and to get the necessary supplies of cash by means of rediscounts, and being thus secured of adequate liquid resources, they were in a position to grant their own customers the necessary breathing space.

marked at the Bank of England. Even if that be deducted the imports were still more than enough to offset the export to Japan.

[1] The following table shows the fall recorded in certain commodities :—

AVERAGE PRICE FOR MONTH.

		May.	November.	Fall per Cent.
Corn	per bushel	1·98	0·80	59
Wheat (spring) . .	,,	3·07½	1·75¼	53
,, (winter) . .	,,	2·97½	2·05¾	31
Hides	per lb.	0·35	0·23	34
Wool	,,	1·16	0·69	41
Coffee	,,	0·15½	0·07½	52
Sugar	,,	0·22½	0·09½	58

Some commodities showed little or no fall, but the foregoing list includes so many important staples of which the stocks to be held are large, that the effect of their decline in value upon the credit situation is obvious.

The situation was surmounted, not without casualties, but without a panic.

The appreciation of the dollar in terms of commodities was reflected in the foreign exchanges. The fall in the exchanges which took place in February had been confined to Europe. The fall in November, while it brought some of the European currencies lower than in February, was general. It extended to South America and to the East. Japan alone, the only surviving companion of the United States in the maintenance of the gold standard, stood outside. The extent of the fall varied. Sterling, which had recovered to $4 in the spring, fell to $3·35 or 16 per cent. Somewhat similar declines were recorded in the case of the stronger European ex-neutrals, Switzerland, Holland, and Sweden. This drop fell so far short of the proportion in which the commodity value of the dollar had risen that it supplies evidence of the success of deflationary measures in those countries. Other currencies showed falls of 30, 40, or even 50 per cent. Some of the collapsed currencies of Eastern Europe fell more than 50 per cent. The Argentine exchange was still at par in the middle of July, but the export of gold was prohibited, and by November the peso was depreciated 20 per cent. The price of silver, which in April averaged $1·20½ (and had been higher), fell to $0·78½ in November, and of course the Chinese exchanges moved with it. The rupee fell from 49½ cents to 26¼ cents.

These movements of the exchanges become more intelligible when it is realised that the purchasing power of the dollar was raised between May and December in the proportion almost of three to two. The apparent depreciation of other currencies for the most part merely measured the appreciation of the gold dollar, the standard by which they were measured. The torrent of forced liquidation that depressed prices in the home markets drove with equal force against foreign markets. But there, instead of bringing down prices, it brought down the exchanges. The effect was the same; the flood of sales was checked, and kept within the absorptive power of the markets.

Is it possible, one is tempted to ask, that such mighty changes can be wrought by so simple and slight an instrument as a rise in the discount rate by about 2 per cent.? Yes, it is. It is possible, first of all, because the rise in the rate broke the vicious circle of inflation; secondly, and still more, because it set up a new vicious circle of deflation. The principle in both cases is the same, though the circumstances of its application are contrary. Deflation once started, prices once on the down grade, the holding of commodities in stock means an actual loss. The prospect of this loss has itself a deterrent effect upon traders, who make a practice of holding commodities with borrowed money, and reinforces the deterrent effect of the rate of discount. In the first instance the rise in discounts discourages dealers from buying and impels them to sell. But the result is so to depress markets that their efforts to sell are ineffectual. The unwillingness of the dealers to buy means fewer orders to producers; profits are smaller, less wages are earned, and thus the consumers' demand shrinks. The rush to sell in an unfavourable market forces down prices, and the fall of prices reinforces the original process. Therefore, once a high discount rate has become deterrent at all, it tends to grow more and more deterrent. In the long and varied experience of the Bank of England in controlling the credit market of London, and therefore of the world, examples are to be found again and again of a very high bank rate being followed as soon as it has done its work, by a very low rate. In 1907 the bank rate was put up to 7 per cent. at the beginning of November. Early in January, 1908, it came down to 6 per cent.; before the end of January it was 4 per cent.; by May it was $2\frac{1}{2}$ per cent.

In 1920 the Federal Reserve Board adhered to the 7 per cent. rate to the end of the year, and the rate on commercial paper remained at or near 8 per cent. The rates that had been imposed in June to counteract the excessive profits of a period of unprecedented inflation were retained when the profits had not merely vanished but had given place to widespread loss and depression.

The turn of the year was safely surmounted. The

maximum reached by the issue of Federal Reserve notes was
$3400 millions on 24th December, and the surplus reserves of
the Federal Reserve banks were then $332 millions. There-
after every factor in the situation conduced to a favourable
reserve position. The note-issue steadily decreased. The
gold reserves, fed by enormous imports, offset by no exports
worth mentioning, grew and grew. By the end of January
the surplus reserve had reached $500 millions, at the end of
March $650 millions, at the end of April $760 millions.
Prices continued to fall. The index number, which was 189
in December, was only 154 in April, or 43½ per cent. below
the maximum of the preceding May. The purchasing power
of the dollar had thus been raised by 80 per cent.

It was not until 5th May that the Federal Reserve Board
relaxed the grip which it had by that time maintained on the
discount market for eleven months. Even then the discount
rate was only reduced to 6½ per cent. Successive reductions
of ½ per cent. at a time gradually brought it down (in New
York) to 4½ per cent. on 3rd November. The price index
reached a minimum of 148 in June and July, and has varied
little since. The first glimmerings of a trade revival can now
be discerned. But meanwhile the effect of the Federal Reserve Board's extremely severe discount policy is to be seen in
the portentous increase of the surplus reserves to $1500
millions.

It will have been noticed that in the foregoing description of
the working of the Federal Reserve system nothing has been
said as to changes in the amount of deposits. The reason is
that the deposit liability of the Federal Reserve banks turned
out not to be an important factor in the calculations. On 7th
March, 1919, the net deposits had already reached $1800
millions, and from that date till July, 1920, oscillated quite
irregularly between $1600 and $1900 millions.[1] Thereafter it
found a somewhat lower average level, but without falling
appreciably below $1600 millions. The amount of deposits
was substantially less than the amount of Federal Reserve

[1] A drop to $1500 millions on 19th September may be disregarded. It was
due to exceptional and transitory causes.

notes, and their cyclical variations were far less, while the proportion of reserve required against them was only 35 per cent.
Their chief importance arose from their day-to-day variations,
a change of $100 millions between one week's return and the
next being not uncommon.   To understand the movements
in the Federal Reserve banks' deposits it is best to turn to
the returns of the Member banks.

MEMBER BANKS.

DEPOSITS AND RESERVES.

($ millions.)

Date.	Deposits.		Reserves.
	Demand.	Time.	
31 December, 1918 . . .	17,103	3,834	1,655
4 March, 1919	16,506	4,092	1,633
30 June, 1919	17,550	4,343	1,724
17 November, 1919 . . .	19,717	5,049	1,825
31 December, 1919 . . .	20,154	5,305	1,904
4 May, 1920	18,876	5,748	1,866
30 June, 1920	19,177	5,911	1,839
15 November, 1920 . . .	18,696	6,144	1,827
29 December, 1920 . . .	17,676	6,188	1,763
28 April, 1921	16,174	6,343	1,654
30 June, 1921	16,544	6,367	1,625

In all the weekly returns of the Federal Reserve banks
themselves from January, 1919, to December, 1921, the
maximum of the member banks' reserve deposits was $1943
millions (on 16th January, 1920) and the minimum was
$1563 millions (on 20th February, 1919).   The whole range
of variations was thus $380 millions, the range in the re-
quired reserve being 35 per cent. of this, or $133 millions.
In the same period the Federal Reserve note issue rose from
$2450 millions in January, 1919, to a maximum of $3404
millions in December, 1920, and fell to $2366 millions at the
end of November, 1921.   The range of $1038 millions means
a range in the required reserve of $415 millions.

Seeing that the total cash reserves of the Federal Reserve
banks fell from a maximum of $2270 millions on 6th June,

1919, to a minimum of $2035 millions on 20th February, 1920, and rose to $3000 millions in December, 1921, it is obvious that at any rate under recent conditions the most potent influence on the Federal Reserve system has been the demand for currency.

Let us therefore turn to consider the effect of the system as a whole upon the currency position. The following analysis of the distribution of money (in $ millions) in the United States in June of each year brings out the changes clearly :—

Date.	In Treasury.	Federal Reserve Banks.	Other Banks.[1]	Public Circulation.
1914 . .	336·3	—	1,630·0	1,772·0
1915 . .	345·4	386·2	1,447·9	1,809·9
1916 . .	298·2	592·7	1,472·2	2,119·8
1917 . .	268·4	1,280·9	1,487·3	2,371·4
1918 . .	360·3	2,018·4	882·7	3,479·6
1919 . .	584·2	2,167·3	981·3	3,786·0
1920 . .	489·7	2,021·3	1,047·3	4,336·2
1921 . .	460·6	2,697·5	946·0	3,920·0

In the first place we see from the column headed " Other Banks " the effect of the reduced reserve requirements. Here a comparison with the total deposits in all banks (except savings banks) in the United States is instructive :—

Date.	Deposits.	Cash.	Ratio.
June, 1914	13,729	1,571	11·44
June, 1915	14,225	1,395	9·80
June, 1916	17,784	1,426	8·02
June, 1917	21,651	1,442	6·66
June, 1918	23,491	839	3·57
June, 1919	27,870	928	3·33
June, 1920	31,462	998	3·17
June, 1921	29,832	898	3·01

The drop from 11·44 per cent. in 1914 to 6·66 per cent. in 1917 shows the progressive effect of the transfer of reserves to the Federal Reserve banks (a process which was spread over three years). The further drop to 3·57 per cent. in 1918 is due to the amending Act of 1917, under which the whole

---

[1] Including savings banks.

statutory reserve has to be on deposit with the Federal
Reserve Bank.

It is of some interest to note that when the cash holdings
of banks, with ample rediscounting facilities open to them, are
reduced to the amount really needed without any effort at
window-dressing, a proportion of about 3 per cent. is found
sufficient.   If a proportion of 11·44 per cent. had been maintained in June, 1921, the total cash holdings would have been
$3400 millions, so that the Federal Reserve system may
fairly be regarded as dispensing with $2500 millions in cash,
which would otherwise have had to lie in the vaults of the
banks.

On the other hand, the member banks have to maintain
their statutory reserves on deposit with the Federal Reserve
banks, which in turn are bound to hold 35 per cent. of those
reserves in cash.   This 35 per cent. has varied between $547
millions and $680 millions.

The mere fact that on balance the Federal Reserve Act
has had an inflationary tendency through the diminution of
statutory cash reserves is not of great importance, because it
is likely enough that in any case inflationary legislation of
some kind would have been passed at the outbreak of war.
But it requires to be borne in mind in making any comparison
between present and pre-war stocks of currency.

As a *continuing* influence on the currency supply the effect
of the system is of course to be found in the absorption of reserves and in the issue of Federal Reserve notes.   Broadly
speaking, no doubt, the great fluctuations in the note issue,
which I have already mentioned, reflect fluctuations in the
demand for currency.   But the correspondence is not exact.
The supply of currency may also be affected by variations
both in the supply of gold and in the reserves of the Federal
Reserve banks themselves.   If the currency in circulation (i.e.
in banks other than Federal Reserve banks, and in the hands
of the public) be divided into Federal Reserve notes and other
kinds of money it will be found that from April, 1917, to
April, 1919, the latter steadily declined from $3744 millions
to $2338 millions, while the Federal Reserve notes rose from

$357 millions to $2503 millions, the net increase in money of all kinds being $740 millions.

But since 1st April, 1919, the variations in other kinds of money have been relatively small, the maximum and minimum being $2348 millions and $2118 millions, although the total has risen from $4800 millions to $5600 millions and fallen again to $4600 millions. It would seem, therefore, that variations in the demand for currency are mainly met by variations in the supply of Federal Reserve notes. At the same time the effect of the big gold movements has been concentrated in the Federal Reserve banks' cash reserves.

Undoubtedly these operations carry out faithfully one of the purposes of the Federal Reserve Act, the provision of an elastic currency. But there is a curious want of logic in the system, which might quite possibly take tangible form in practical disadvantages. Federal Reserve notes are not legal tender, and there is no particular reason why any one should prefer them to gold or silver certificates or United States notes, which are " lawful money." The proportion of Federal Reserve notes to other money in circulation is really a matter of caprice. The banks may thrust them on their customers, as a conjurer forces a card, but a very slight preference on the part of the customers might break the spell and completely upset the reserve position. Or, on the other hand, when the reserves are falling low, the banks may resort again to the conjurer's art to put Federal Reserve notes in circulation in place of other forms of money. Though anything in the nature of a concerted discrimination by the public against the notes is hardly a serious danger, there is undoubtedly an element of arbitrariness in having the new currency and the old in circulation side by side. The anomaly would have been avoided if the Federal Reserve note-issue had been based on the principle of a fixed fiduciary issue, as under the Bank Charter Act of 1844, instead of a fixed proportion of gold reserve. No doubt, the fixed proportion was preferred as being more " elastic."

This property of elasticity in currency, which was one of the avowed purposes of the Federal Reserve Act, deserves examination. A currency needs elasticity for two purposes. It must be readily adaptable to seasonal demands, and it must be expansible to meet an exceptional emergency such as a crisis. For seasonal demands the margin of gold in excess of the statutory reserves at the time of minimum demand must be sufficient to leave some margin still in existence when the demand has grown to the maximum, and here there is undoubtedly some advantage in the fixed proportion system. With a fixed fiduciary issue, the whole of the additional notes outstanding at the time of maximum demand must be covered, dollar for dollar, with gold. If at that time the margin of reserves, above the legal limit, is adequate for contingencies, then at the time of minimum demand it will be much more than adequate.

On the other hand, if the gold reserve is required to be a fixed proportion of the issue, for example 40 per cent., then the margin at the time of minimum demand will only be swollen by that fraction of the additional issue. For example, in 1920 the Federal Reserve note-issue increased by $300 millions between June and December. With a fixed fiduciary issue it would have been necessary to have an extra reserve of the whole amount of $300 millions to prepare for the increase, whereas with the 40 per cent. proportion laid down by the Federal Reserve Act only $120 millions were required.

But when it comes to meeting the exceptional demand for currency in a time of crisis, the arithmetical rule for the calculation of reserves becomes irrelevant. The occurrence of the crisis itself presupposes that the reserve is at or near the limit. The only remedy then may be to suspend the limit. The aim of a sound banking system is to maintain such a control of credit as will avoid this necessity altogether, or will, if it does occur, ensure the earliest possible return to the normal compliance with the law.

For this vital purpose of controlling credit the fixed proportion system of reserves offers some specious advantages which on examination turn out to be illusory. When credit is unduly relaxed, the effect of the consequent expansion of the currency upon the surplus reserve is reduced in the

proportion adopted.   If the proportion is 40 per cent., every
$100 added to the circulation diminishes the surplus reserve
by $40.   So long as the reserve proportion is taken as the
criterion of the credit position, this facilitates expansion.

But when the expansion produces its natural consequence
of an export of gold, and a contraction in the currency becomes
necessary, the contraction required to make good a given loss
of gold is *increased* in the same proportion.   As a result, in
the critical interval before the export of gold has been checked,
the contraction is all the more likely to be so violent as to
provoke a crisis.

The decisive moment is likely to come at or near the
period of maximum seasonal demand for currency, and, if it
does, even the elasticity which facilitates provision for that
demand is likely to prove treacherous.   In the control of
credit what is needed above all is prompt action.   Credit is
unstable, and a movement once started, whether it be an
expansion or contraction, gathers impetus till it is checked.
Delay always aggravates the evil, and an elastic currency
facilitates delay.   That one vital fault outweighs all its
advantages.

If in practice the danger can be avoided, that is because
in any case the authority controlling credit must exercise
discretion; it cannot rely on any rule of thumb.   Neither a
fixed proportion nor a fixed fiduciary issue is an infallible
guide.   The Federal Reserve Board must exercise unceasing
vigilance.   It is not even enough to watch price movements,
important as they are.   All the symptoms of the state of
credit and of trade must be observed, and the Board must be
ready to anticipate and as far as possible to prevent any
movement from the normal.

In America, as here, the note-issue is but a small part of
the total stock of purchasing power.   Table III enables us to
trace the history of bank deposits during the critical period
following the armistice.   The two returns of 31st December,
1918, and 4th March, 1919, show no appreciable change in
deposits as compared with that of 1st November, 1918.   Investments show a large increase from $8759 to $10,082 millions,

but this was partly set off by a drop in loans and discounts. Thereupon there began a rapid increase in deposits from $25,542 millions in March to $31,677 millions on 31st December, 1919, or 24 per cent. Concurrently there was a *decrease* in investments to $9125 millions, and a rise in loans and discounts from $19,359 to $24,492 millions. The pressure on banking funds for direct investment in Government securities was already over, and the expansion was in ordinary banking accommodation to trade. In the following eleven months to November, 1920, there was no further increase in deposits, which stood at $31,671 millions, but the substitution of loans and discounts for investments continued. Thus, the increase in deposits in the post-armistice expansion may be estimated at 24 per cent. The increase in money in circulation was from $4841 millions on 1st April, 1919, to $5381 millions on 1st July, 1920, or only 11 per cent. Prices on the contrary rose from 200 in March, 1919, to 272 in May, 1920, or 36 per cent.

Between November, 1920, and April, 1921, deposits fell to $28,995 millions or 8½ per cent. But by June, 1921, they had recovered somewhat and the fall was only 6 per cent., while prices fell from 269 to 148 or 45 per cent. The money in circulation from $5381 millions on 1st July, 1920, continued rising for a few months, reached a maximum of $5617 millions on 1st November, and stood at $4866 millions on 1st July, showing a fall on balance of 10 per cent. in the year. Here we have an illustration of the rule that when business is active prices rise more than in proportion to the stock of purchasing power, and that when business is slack they fall more than in proportion. In other words, when business is active the rapidity of circulation is increased, and when business is slack it is diminished. Stagnant cash balances are a characteristic of periods of trade depression. When trade is profitable, dealers cannot afford to let money lie idle, but when every transaction threatens, under the stress of falling markets, to end in a loss, idle balances are allowed to mount up. In the one case every one is a bull of commodities and a bear of currency; in the other every one is a bear of commodities and a bull of currency.

This phenomenon has been exemplified in an even more

striking form in this country.   A deflation so intense as to
reduce prices of commodities by nearly 50 per cent. and to
throw 2,000,000 people out of employment has been accompanied by no visible fall in bank deposits.   And it is even
argued that there has been no deflation at all, as if the
quantity of purchasing power were the sole test of the state of
credit.   The kind of deflation that is practically important is
deflation not of the outstanding aggregate of purchasing
power but of the *flow* of purchasing power.

If we review the experience of the last three years we shall
find, I think, that the Federal Reserve Act has conferred an
incalculable benefit upon America, in that it has successfully
set up an authority with the special duty of exercising fore-
sight and initiative in the regulation of credit.   The Federal
Reserve Board, which is a judicious blend of Government and
business representation, has discharged its functions during a
period of unexampled difficulty with such skill and with such
public spirit as to gain the confidence and goodwill of the
banking world.

Nevertheless, to avoid mistakes altogether in such circumstances would be something more than human, and it is already
possible to draw instructive conclusions from the experience
that has been acquired.   In the first place, the inflationary
movement, which began in the spring of 1919 and brought
about a rise in prices of 38 per cent., was ultimately checked
by a rise in rediscount rates.   Could it not have been checked
at an earlier stage?   The Federal Reserve Board seems to have
been infected with that scepticism as to the efficacy of the
rediscount rate which has been so prevalent since the war.
Till November, 1919, it is true, they found an obstacle to action
in the position of the banks which had undertaken to grant
advances at low rates to subscribers to war loans.   It seemed
unfair to charge these banks such high rates for rediscounts as
to involve them in a loss.   And, moreover, "an advance in
discount rates, while the Government had an unwieldy floating
debt, and Liberty Bonds were still largely unabsorbed, would
have added to the difficulties of Government financing."

But after November, 1919, these motives ceased to operate,

and yet six months passed before effective steps were taken to stop the credit expansion. "The purchasing power of the public," said the Board, in their report of 1919, "growing out of high wages and large profits, is greater than it has ever been before; and this purchasing power . . . has raised prices to a point that takes no account of prudence." Yet it was only by tentative and hesitating steps that the Board tried to cope with this menacing situation, and it was not till 1st June, 1920, that the rediscount rate was raised to 7 per cent. That measure was successful, and the tide turned, but the ebb had to be proportioned to the flow. In so far as the expansion had got out of hand, the subsequent contraction had to be more severe.

By the end of the year the prices of commodities had already fallen below the minimum of 1919, and the whole of the ground lost had thus been regained. That there was no crisis or panic is to be put down to the credit of the Federal Reserve system, and of the Board which administered it. But the other ill-effects of a rapid credit contraction, in the form of loss and unemployment, were experienced to the full.

We have already seen how during 1921 the transition from dear to cheap money was delayed. In America the delay meant an intensification and prolongation of the industrial distress. But its results were not confined to America. All over the world the currency situation was profoundly disturbed, owing to the fact that the value of the dollar, that is to say, of gold, in relation to commodities was raised by no less than 80 per cent. The financially strong countries in Western Europe elected to adopt the same severe deflationary methods as the United States, and had to suffer the same distress. The financially weak saw their currencies apparently depreciating. All thought of stabilisation had to be put aside.

It may be said that even now a dollar is only worth two-thirds as much as in 1913, and that it is hardly the business of other nations to complain if the Americans have thought it desirable to make this partial return to pre-war standards. There would be force in this contention if there were a prospect of the dollar being permanently stabilised at that point. But the original depreciation of the dollar to less than two-fifths of its pre-war commodity value was caused by the influx of a flood of gold, and now the gold is there in larger volume than ever.

Going back to the table on p. 114 we see that in 1914 of the $3738 millions of money of all kinds, $1772 millions were in the hands of the public, outside the banks. In June, 1921, the money in the hands of the public had risen to $3920 millions, an increase of 121 per cent. Bank deposits had increased from $13,729 millions to $29,832 millions, or 117 per cent. After all allowances have been made for the increased need for currency in a growing community with growing wealth, it seems obvious that this supply of purchasing power is more than sufficient to support a 50 per cent. increase of prices. And, in fact, the disproportion is one more piece of evidence of the stagnation of cash balances characteristic of a period of depression. As soon as there is a revival the flow of purchasing power will be increased, although the outstanding aggregate will be stationary or may even diminish. But that is not all. Even with this excessive supply of purchasing power in circulation, the reserves of the Federal Reserve banks are also swollen far beyond normal proportions. The surplus reserve was already practically $1000 millions in June. Now it exceeds $1500 millions.

The appreciation of gold has effectively prevented other countries from restoring the gold standard, and the entire surplus gold supply of the world has been persistently gravitating towards the United States. So long as this state of things continues, the reserve proportions established by the Federal Reserve Act will be entirely inoperative. In other words, the Federal Reserve system itself points the way to another great inflationary movement. When that movement becomes perceptible, however, it will meet with conditions in some other countries very different from those of 1919. For two years Western Europe has been striving after a gold standard, and in the effort has by this time sustained an even more severe deflation than the United States. In this country the discount on the currency has been reduced to 8 per cent.

In Sweden and Holland it is less.   In Switzerland the franc has already been at par with gold.   A moderate inflation in America will depreciate the dollar to the level of sterling, and gold exports for currency purposes will become possible to England and to the Continent.   As credit expansion proceeds, other countries (e.g. Japan, and perhaps Argentina, Uruguay, Spain, or Denmark) may be put in a position to take gold.   Thus may the gold standard be spread and the redundant gold reserves of the United States be drawn off by the simple expedient of cheapening gold in the world market.

But if that is to happen in the future, why was gold ever made dear?   We have been made familiar by Prof. Cassel and Prof. Irving Fisher with the importance of stabilising the currency unit, and the experience of the Federal Reserve Board has supplied them with their most telling example. The whole world has been plunged into the most appalling distress for nearly two years by the strain of raising the commodity value of the dollar 80 per cent.   And now a great part of what has been done is about to be undone!   To that extent the effort was pure waste.   It was indeed worse, for the undoing is itself, as we well know, a process full of danger.

How did such a mistake ever come to be made?   The explanation is, I think, simply that the working of the " vicious circle " of deflation was not understood.   It was not realised that a deterrent rediscount rate, once it has taken effect, can safely be reduced, and that the falling prices and shrinking purchasing power will then do their work without extraneous aid.

Credit is inherently unstable, and it can only be successfully controlled by perpetual vigilance and prompt action. Every disturbance from the normal, whether towards expansion or towards contraction, tends to magnify itself unless quickly checked by the appropriate rise or fall in the discount rate.   Traders and bankers often deprecate rapid changes in the discount rate as being unsettling to business.   But what is unsettling is the alternation between expanding and contracting credit.   If credit, and therefore the flow of purchasing power, are kept approximately steady, the short-period changes in the rate of discount cause no trouble except in the highly specialised calculations of the discount market itself.

Another lesson to be derived from the period we have been studying is the extent of the command which those who regulate credit have over the commodity value of gold. This, of course, is not new. It is the very foundation of the theory of bimetallism. But the practical experience of the Federal Reserve Board shows that the purchasing power of a gold unit can be fixed anywhere within fairly wide limits, and that the gold supply will accommodate itself to the value chosen. This points the way to the much desired stabilisation of the unit.

TABLE I.—FEDERAL RESERVE BANKS.

(Millions of dollars.)

Date.	Deposits.	Federal Reserve Notes.	Required Reserve.	Actual Reserve.			Surplus Reserve.
				Gold.	Other Cash.	Total.	
27 Nov., 1914	249·3	2·7	88·3	227·8	34·6	262·4	174·1
26 Nov., 1915	398·9	165·3	205·7	492·2	37·2	529·4	323·7
24 Nov., 1916	650·7	275·3	337·9	736·2	17·6	753·8	415·9
25 May, 1917	721·2	454·4	434·2	977·4	36·9	1,014·3	580·1
29 June, 1917	1,261·8	508·7	645·1	1,294·5	39·8	1,334·3	689·2
28 Dec., 1917	1,458·0	1,246·5	1,008·9	1,671·1	49·6	1,720·7	711·9
28 June, 1918	1,529·8	1,722·2	1,224·3	1,949·0	57·2	2,006·2	781·9
1 Nov., 1918	1,663·4	2,515·5	1,588·4	2,052·2	53·5	2,105·7	517·3
27 Dec., 1918	1,552·9	2,685·2	1,617·6	2,090·3	55·9	2,146·2	528·6
7 Mar., 1919	1,802·1	2,488·5	1,626·1	2,139·5	66·0	2,205·5	579·3
27 June, 1919	1,750·7	2,499·2	1,612·4	2,147·8	68·4	2,216·2	603·8
14 Nov., 1919	1,858·3	2,808·4	1,773·8	2,133·3	66·8	2,200·1	426·3
26 Dec., 1919	1,704·5	3,057·6	1,819·6	2,078·4	57·1	2,135·5	315·9
14 May, 1920	1,839·4	3,083·2	1,877·1	1,939·1	139·3	2,078·4	201·3
25 June, 1920	1,722·2	3,116·7	1,849·5	1,969·4	139·2	2,108·6	259·1
12 Nov., 1920	1,674·8	3,329·0	1,917·8	2,008·7	171·3	2,180·0	262·2
30 Dec., 1920	1,604·2	3,344·7	1,899·3	2,059·4	189·8	2,249·2	349·8
27 April, 1921	1,725·9	2,830·1	1,736·1	2,317·6	187·2	2,504·8	768·7
29 June, 1921	1,685·8	2,634·5	1,633·8	2,461·9	163·5	2,625·4	991·6

Note to Table I.—The dates selected are, for the first three years, at annual intervals from the inauguration of the system in November, 1914. In 1917, returns are given just before and just after the amending Act of June, 1917, became operative. Thereafter dates have been taken close to those of the returns of member banks (*see* Tables II and III).

In March, 1921, the method of calculation of deposits for the purposes of the reserve proportion was altered. Till then *net* deposits were taken, that is to say, the F.R. banks were allowed to set off against the gross deposits the net sums due to them through their clearing operations. This is always a positive quantity, because a cheque while in transit to the bank upon which it is drawn is counted as a credit by each bank that it reaches in the clearing chain before it is counted as a debit by the next. In the return for 27th April, 1921, credits included "uncollected items" to the amount of $519·8 millions, and the corresponding debit was $430·7 millions. The difference was $89·1 millions, and under the old system of reckoning would have reduced the deposits to $1,636·8 millions *net*. The difference amounted in the return for 30th December, 1920, to $194·6 millions, making the gross deposits $1,798·8 millions. The new system of reckoning would then have reduced the surplus reserve from $349·8 millions to $281·7 millions.

TABLE II.—BANKING CAPITAL.

(Millions of dollars.)

Date.	Non-National Banks.				National Banks.	All Member Banks.	All Banks.
	Total.	Member Banks.	Others.	Proportion of Member Banks.			
				Per cent.			
30 June, 1914 .	984	—	984	—	1,058	—	2,042
30 June, 1915 .	1,002	9	993	0·9	1,069	1,078	2,071
30 June, 1916 .	1,056	19	1,037	1·8	1,066	1,085	2,122
20 June, 1917 .	1,123	40	1,083	3·56	1,083	1,123	2,206
31 Dec., 1917 .	1,155	218	937	18·87	1,093	1,311	2,248
10 May, 1918 .	1,176	270	906	22·96	1,097	1,367	2,273
29 June, 1918 .	1,184	282	902	23·82	1,099	1,381	2,283
1 Nov., 1918 .	1,209	334	875	27·63	1,108	1,442	2,317
31 Dec., 1918 .	1,221	349	872	28·58	1,110	1,459	2,331
4 March, 1919 .	1,233	360	873	29·20	1,106	1,466	2,339
30 June, 1919 .	1,256	371	885	29·62	1,119	1,490	2,375
17 Nov., 1919 .	1,315	412	903	31·41	1,154	1,566	2,469
31 Dec., 1919 .	1,333	436	897	32·71	1,158	1,594	2,491
4 May, 1920 .	1,385	481	904	34·74	1,215	1,696	2,600
30 June, 1920 .	1,409	493	916	34·99	1,224	1,717	2,633
15 Nov., 1920 .	1,477	518	959	35·07	1,270	1,788	2,747
29 Dec., 1920 .	1,499	528	971	35·22	1,272	1,800	2,771
28 April, 1921 .	1,559	579	980	37·14	1,271	1,850	2,830
30 June, 1921 .	1,590	585	1,005	36·86	1,274	1,859	2,864

Note to Table II.—For national banks and other member banks the amount of capital is taken from the returns made at the end of June and at irregular intermediate dates. For other banks the amount in June of each year is taken from the annual returns of all banks in the United States, and at intermediate dates the total capital of all banks *other than National* has been assumed to increase at an equal rate throughout the year.

TABLE III.—ALL BANKS EXCEPT SAVINGS BANKS.

(Millions of dollars.)

Date.	Loans and Discounts.	Government Securities and Investments.[1]	Cash.	Individual Deposits.[2]
30 June, 1914—				
National banks	6,445	1,810	1,022	6,336
Other banks	5,939	1,665	549	7,393
Total	12,384	3,475	1,571	13,729
23 June, 1915—				
National banks	6,665	2,068	858	6,611
Other Member banks	55	19	4	66
Total Member banks	6,720	2,087	862	6,677
Other banks	6,016	1,766	533	7,548
Total	12,736	3,853	1,395	14,225
30 June, 1916—				
National banks	7,685	2,351	819	8,143
Other Member banks	197	32	14	252
Total Member banks	7,882	2,383	833	8,395
Other banks	7,037	2,280	593	9,389
Total	14,919	4,663	1,426	17,784
20 June, 1917—				
National banks	8,828	3,013	753	9,655
Other Member banks	424	122	38	646
Total Member banks	9,252	3,135	791	10,301
Other banks	8,118	2,578	651	11,350
Total	17,370	5,713	1,442	21,651
29 June, 1918—				
National banks	9,633	3,957	383	11,220
Other Member banks	3,029	1,448	99	4,450
Total	12,662	5,405	482	15,670
Members next June	737	353	24	1,081
Total	13,399	5,758	506	16,751
Other banks	5,558	1,611	333	6,740
Total	18,957	7,369	839	23,491

[1] Including United States Certificates of Indebtedness.
[2] Including United States Government deposits.

TABLE III.—*continued.*

(Millions of dollars.)

Date.	Loans and Discounts.	Government Securities and Investments.[1]	Cash.	Individual Deposits.[2]
1 November, 1918—				
National banks	10,114	4,922	444	12,151
Other Member banks	3,644	1,753	127	5,224
Members next June	262	126	9	376
Total	14,020	6,801	580	17,751
Other banks	5,954	1,941	382	7,453
Total	19,974	8,742	962	25,204
31 December, 1918—				
National banks	9,931	4,740	522	12,248
Other Member banks	3,634	1,823	154	5,373
Members next June	132	67	6	195
Total	13,697	6,630	682	17,816
Other banks	5,883	1,902	449	7,635
Total	19,580	8,532	1,131	25,451
4 March, 1919—				
National banks	9,705	5,491	435	12,094
Other Member banks	3,735	2,294	129	5,590
Members next June	54	33	2	80
Total	13,494	7,818	566	17,764
Other banks	5,865	2,264	373	7,778
Total	19,359	10,082	939	25,542
30 June, 1919—				
National banks	10,589	5,048	424	12,940
Other Member banks	4,323	2,018	136	6,211
Total	14,912	7,066	560	19,151
Members next June	784	366	25	1,126
Total	15,696	7,432	585	20,277
Other banks	5,837	2,009	343	7,593
Total	21,533	9,441	928	27,870
17 November, 1919—				
National banks	11,583	4,865	450	14,097
Other Member banks	5,053	2,075	154	6,983
Members next June	576	236	18	796
Total	17,212	7,176	622	21,876
Other banks	6,838	2,152	369	8,695
Total	24,050	9,328	991	30,571

[1] Including United States Certificates of Indebtedness.
[2] Including United States Government deposits.

TABLE III.—*continued.*

(Millions of dollars.)

Date.	Loans and Discounts.	Government Securities and Investments.[1]	Cash.	Individual Deposits.[2]
31 December, 1919—				
National banks	11,803	4,700	509	14,517
Other Member banks	5,255	2,112	183	7,506
Members next June	366	145	13	523
Total	17,424	6,966	705	22,546
Other banks	7,068	2,158	418	9,130
Total	24,492	9,124	1,123	31,676
4 May, 1920—				
National banks	12,305	4,324	456	13,985
Other Member banks	5,515	2,028	166	7,310
Members next June	40	15	1	52
Total	17,860	6,367	623	21,347
Other banks	7,672	2,163	375	9,122
Total	25,532	8,530	998	30,469
30 June, 1920—				
National banks	12,413	4,186	450	14,311
Other Member banks	5,689	1,977	172	7,582
Total	18,102	6,163	622	21,893
Members next June	318	111	10	424
Total	18,420	6,274	632	22,317
Other banks	7,687	2,073	366	9,152
Total	26,107	8,347	998	31,469
15 November, 1920—				
National banks	12,331	4,106	448	14,313
Other Member banks	5,719	1,950	164	7,552
Members next June	292	99	8	385
Total	18,342	6,155	620	22,250
Other banks	7,929	2,145	385	9,421
Total	26,271	8,300	1,005	31,671
29 December, 1920—				
National banks	12,112	4,122	494	13,732
Other Member banks	5,646	2,010	184	7,393
Members next June	263	93	8	344
Total	18,021	6,225	686	21,469
Other banks	7,879	2,207	435	9,186
Total	25,900	8,432	1,121	30,655

[1] Including United States Certificates of Indebtedness.
[2] Including United States Government deposits.

TABLE III.—*continued*.

(Millions of dollars.)

Date.	Loans and Discounts.	Government Securities and Investments.[1]	Cash.	Individual Deposits.[2]
28 April, 1921—				
National banks	11,378	3,993	402	12,716
Other Member banks	5,815	2,049	163	7,386
Total	17,193	6,042	565	20,132
Other banks	7,751	2,298	380	8,863
Total	24,944	8,340	945	28,995
30 June, 1921—				
National banks	11,135	4,025	374	12,991
Other Member banks	5,775	2,083	156	7,627
Total	16,910	6,108	530	20,618
Other banks	7,747	2,327	368	9,214
Total	24,657	8,435	898	29,832

Note.—For all banks in June of each year and for all member banks (national and other) at intermediate dates, the figures are taken from the published returns.

To estimate the figures for non-member banks at intermediate dates the following method has been adopted :—

In the first place, the figures for member banks at successive dates are not an accurate index of the position of all banks, because the growth of membership disturbs the comparison. To arrive at figures at each intermediate date comparable to those for the member banks in the following June, the non-national member banks (among which alone this growth of membership can occur) have been separated from the national banks. Table II shows what proportion the capital of the non-national member banks bears at each date to the capital of all non-national banks, and from this it is possible to calculate what proportional addition must be made to the capital of the former at any date in order that it may bear the same ratio to the capital of the latter at a subsequent date; e.g. on 17th November, 1919, 31·41 per cent. of the capital of non-national banks belonged to member banks and on 30th June, 1920, 34·99 per cent. If the member capital at the former date had been 11·40 per cent. more it would have amounted to the same proportion as at the latter date, viz. 34·99 per cent. As a first approximation, it may be supposed that such an increase of capital would have meant a proportional increase in each of the other figures (loans and discounts, investments, cash and deposits). This increase, which may be regarded as an estimate of the adjustment required in respect of those banks about to become members between 17th November, 1919, and 30th June, 1920, makes the figures for member banks comparable at the two dates. In

---

[1] Including United States Certificates of Indebtedness.
[2] Including United States Government deposits.

TABLE IV.—AVERAGE RATE OF REDISCOUNT.

one case (28th April, 1921) no adjustment is required because the proportion of the capital of member banks among non-national banks was practically the same as in the following June (see Table II). For those banks which were still not members in the following June, it has been assumed that each item varies at each intermediate date in the same proportion as the corresponding item for all member banks, but upon these variations there has been superimposed another factor to allow for the rate of increase or decrease from one June return to the next, where this rate of increase or decrease is different from that shown by the member banks.

Average rate of discount on paper actually discounted by the Federal Reserve banks in each month since the Armistice.

—	New York.	All Banks.	—	New York.	All Banks.
1918—			**1920—**		
November .	4·09	4·20	May . .	5·56	5·74
December .	4·05	4·18	June . .	6·19	6·20
1919—			July . .	6·25	6·21
January . .	4·07	4·18	August .	6·25	6·19
February .	4·03	4·14	September .	6·47	6·39
March . .	4·02	4·15	October .	6·47	6·40
April . .	4·03	4·18	November .	6·41	6·45
May . .	4·03	4·16	December .	6·51	6·48
June . .	4·04	4·19			
July . .	4·06	4·14	**1921—**		
August .	4·05	4·12	January . .	6·53	6·36
September .	4·04	4·18	February .	6·55	6·41
October .	4·03	4·19	March . .	6·52	6·43
November .	4·49	4·53	April . .	6·45	6·32
December .	4·63	4·67	May . .	6·26	6·22
1920—			June . .	6·15	6·13
January .	4·86	4·90	July . .	5·84	6·02
February .	5·42	5·52	August .	5·50	5·76
March . .	5·53	5·64	September .	5·33	5·75
April . .	5·48	5·67	October .	5·00	5·62

VI.

THE GENOA RESOLUTIONS ON CURRENCY.

THE Financial Commission of the Genoa Conference passed a series of twelve Resolutions (Cmd. 1667, pp. 60-2) on the subject of currency which were adopted by the full Conference, and which may therefore be regarded as the united voice of the Governments of Europe.

That there should really be twelve propositions on the subject of currency, which command the agreement of all Europe, would seem to be a fantasy hardly deserving serious consideration. That there should even be the appearance of agreement invites the suspicion that the resolutions must be strictly confined to pious platitudes, and surely the stock of pious platitudes respecting currency must long ago have been exhausted, if not at the Brussels Conference of 1920, at any rate at the multitudinous conferences and discussions which have taken place since the end of the war.

By most critics the Genoa Resolutions are dismissed with some such remarks as these. And there is no difficulty in supporting their criticisms with quotations from the resolutions themselves. That stability is desirable, that Central banks should be independent of political pressure, that all European currencies should be based on a common standard, that the only possible common standard is gold, that, so long as budget deficits are met by the creation of paper money, currency reform is impossible, these are propositions of the familiar type.

But to suppose that all the resolutions conform to this model is to do them something less than justice, and in the following pages I shall endeavour to show what is their practical bearing, and what results we may hope for from them.

The first practical step recommended in the resolutions is the meeting of representatives of Central banks (Res. 3), to be summoned by the Bank of England (Res. 12), to which representatives of the United States are to be invited (Res. 10). The primary object of this meeting is to develop " the practice of continuous co-operation among Central banks of issue, or banks regulating credit policy in the several countries " (Res. 3), but there is specifically referred to it a scheme for an international convention, based on a gold exchange standard, and designed " with a view to preventing undue fluctuations in the purchasing power of gold " (Res. 11).

Another international conference! What, will the line stretch out to the crack of doom?

But here there is a difference. The calling in of the Central banks is a recognition of the principle that currency policy is ultimately credit policy, for the direction of credit policy is the special function of a Central bank.

It is true that the currency inflation during the war, and the most flagrant examples of currency inflation since, have been due to the action, not of Central banks, but of Governments. If the Central banks contributed, that was only because they were allowed no choice but to create credit for their Governments.

It is everywhere recognised that Government action of this kind must cease if anything whatever is to be done with the currency, and some of the pious platitudes adopted at Genoa (Resns. 2, 7, and 11 (1) (a)) were needed to place this presupposition on record once again.

If the Conference added nothing to what had already been said on this topic, that was because there was nothing to add. The particular measures required for balancing budgets and avoiding inflationary finance are not, properly speaking, currency measures at all, though they are very intimately affected by the state of the currency. Moreover, except in one important but limited class of cases, they provide no field for international action. They are the domestic business of each country, and are not the concern of an international conference. With regard to the exception, the inter-government obligations left behind by the Great War, we shall have a word to say later on.

Inflationary Government finance once eliminated, the real responsibility for the currency passes from the Government to the Central bank.   The Central bank may be itself a Government department, or essentially subordinate to the Government, but, even if it is, it has the responsibility for regulating the currency *on banking principles*.   When therefore the Governments of Europe pass on their monetary programme to the Central banks, it is the same sort of step forward as is taken by allies in war when the political leaders hand over the task of concerting operations to the military commanders.   Broad guidance must be given by the political leaders, but it is only the military commanders who can plan and take practical action.

When the supply of paper money through advances to the Government for budget expenses is cut off, the banking and trading community can only get fresh supplies of currency from the Central bank through the instrumentality of trade borrowing, such as discounts and advances.   The only means of regulating the supply of currency is then by encouraging or discouraging trade borrowing.   Legislative or administrative regulations, limiting or prescribing the issue of legal tender money, may play an important part, but, in the last resort, only by affecting the action of the Central bank.   Anyone who can borrow from the Central bank can thereby procure legal tender money, and in such borrowing operations (which in most countries take the form of rediscounting) is concentrated the whole demand for currency.   If the issues of currency are to be limited, whether by statute or otherwise, practical effect can only be given to the limitation through a control of rediscounts.

In the scheme which is referred to the meeting of Central banks, is embodied the plan of campaign adopted by the Governments at Genoa.   It starts (Res. 11, par. 1) with the necessary governmental and legislative action, viz. : (*a*) the elimination of inflationary methods from the budget, and (*b*) the determination of the gold value of the monetary unit.   The next step, (c) "the gold value so fixed must then be made effective in a free exchange market," is one involving credit regulation, and therefore demands co-operation by the Central bank.   For the determination of the gold value of the monetary unit fixes implicitly a standard for its purchasing power in terms of goods and services.   If the standard diverges from actual market conditions, then the purchasing power of the unit must be modified.   Convertibility into gold or foreign exchange is not practicable until the unit is at or very near the parity determined upon, and thus in the first instance the value of the unit must be adjusted through the Central bank's credit policy.   If the prescribed value is above the existing market value of the unit, credit must be contracted; if below, credit must be relaxed.

Now changes, through credit regulation, in the purchasing power of the unit are not to be made at will and without limit. An undue expansion or contraction of credit, involving a general rise or fall in prices, has detrimental and even disastrous results upon the economic life of the community. Therefore when the legislation is introduced for the second stage, (b) the determination of the gold value of the unit, the Central bank, by whose action alone effect can be given to the decision, must be consulted and must participate.

The fourth step is (d) " the provision of an adequate reserve of approved assets, not necessarily gold."   The reserve will, of course, be the property of the Central bank, which is responsible for using it to maintain the convertibility of the currency. That will not prevent the Government from assisting in various ways, but the principal in the business will be the bank and not the Government.

In fact every stage in the process of returning to the gold standard, except the pre-requisite balancing of the national budget, requires at least the co-operation of the Central bank.

Pars. 2-7 of Res. 11 deal with the subsequent working of the convention, when the gold standard is actually operative. It may be asked, why is any international agreement on the subject of the gold standard necessary at all?   When we have once got a currency based on a commodity like gold, why should we not rely on free market conditions, as we did before the war?

To ask such questions is to disregard the profound changes which have occurred since 1914. The substitution of paper for gold as the circulating medium in so many countries has displaced an enormous amount of gold from circulation. This gold has mostly gone to swell the stock in the United States, being the only country left with a real gold standard. The result has been a great fall in the commodity value of gold. Even now the commodity value of the gold dollar, after being raised 80 per cent. in twelve months by the most severe deflation ever effected, is only two-thirds of what it was before the war. If currency reform means simply a reversion to pre-war conditions, there is an obvious risk that the value of gold may be raised again by "the simultaneous and competitive efforts of countries to secure metallic reserves" (Res. 9). This is not a visionary or theoretical danger. Several examples are to be found in history of the derangement of monetary conditions through an ill-regulated competition for the precious metals. The most notorious is the chronic state of depression which prevailed during the spread of the gold standard in the period 1873-96. A less well-known but still instructive instance is to be found in the breakdown of the return to specie payments in England, Austria-Hungary, and Russia in the period 1816-18, through the depletion of the French reserves of gold and silver and the consequent credit stringency in Paris.

If an undue demand for gold is to be avoided, we must have some method of economising the use of gold as currency. This we find ready to hand in the gold exchange standard, the application of which forms the subject of pars. 2-5 of Res. 11. The principle is that the currency of each participating country, instead of being convertible into gold, may be convertible at par into the currencies of the others. To secure convertibility, the participating countries will hold reserves of "approved assets" (bank balances, bills, short term securities or other suitable liquid resources) in one another's currencies, and will undertake to buy and sell such assets freely for their own currencies.

Different currencies linked by an exchange standard so planned could be maintained permanently at par with one another without the intervention of any metallic medium at all. If the system is to be based on a gold standard, then, at some point or other, one at least of the currencies must be convertible not merely into other currencies but into gold. Accordingly "certain of the participating countries will establish a free market in gold, and thus become gold centres" (par. 2).

At the gold centres some gold reserves must be maintained. But if the convention is practically world-wide, if all the gold-standard countries adhere to it, gold will nowhere be needed as a means of remittance, and gold will only be withdrawn from the reserves for use as a raw material of industry.

The precise extent of the industrial demand is not accurately known, but it can hardly amount to £50,000,000 a year. At any rate, even with the fall since 1914 in the value of gold in comparison with other commodities, it is unlikely that the industrial consumption of gold has so far increased as to approach the annual output, which is now about £70,000,000.

The aggregate gold reserves held for monetary purposes exceed £1,500,000,000. Here we have a "visible supply" of a commodity equal to something like thirty years' consumption. In face of the existence of such a stock, the gold market cannot but be entirely artificial. A release from stock of a quantity of gold, quite moderate in proportion to the total, might completely swamp the market. In fact, the gold exchange standard is *too* effective in economising gold. If it were pushed to its logical limits, far the greater part of the existing gold reserves would become redundant, and the commodity value of gold, upon which the value of every currency unit depends, might be depressed below even the low value which it reached in 1920 (when the purchasing power of the gold dollar fell to $\frac{3}{8}$ of what it had been in 1914).

It is therefore apparent that in tying our currency units to gold, we are not securing a natural or stable standard of value at all. To complete the system, we must provide for the proper regulation of the almost unlimited power which the currency authorities will have over the value of gold itself.

Accordingly "credit will be regulated, not only with a view to maintaining the currencies at par with one another, but also with a view to preventing undue fluctuations in the purchasing power of gold" (Res. 11 (7)).

Critics of the Genoa Resolutions have for the most part either overlooked this recommendation altogether, or they have viewed it with misgiving and suspicion as an academic proposal of doubtful practicability. What has already been said above, shows how essential the stabilisation of gold is to the whole scheme. But it will be worth while to examine it in some detail, in order both to remove misconceptions and to reveal the implications of the proposal.

In the first place, what of its practicability? Can the value of gold be regulated, and, if so, how? With a gold standard, the *price* of gold in currency is fixed, and every one knows how gold reserves can be used to prevent the price varying. What we are here concerned with is the value of gold, and therefore of the currency unit *in terms of other commodities.*

In other words, we want to stabilise prices. Needless to say, it is not suggested that anything should be done to control the prices of particular commodities. The proposal is to eliminate causes tending to raise or lower *all* prices. Such causes proceed from the state of the currency. According to the quantity theory, an increase or decrease in the quantity of means of payment (including both legal tender money, and bank credits subject to cheque) tends to bring about a proportional increase or decrease in prices. The supply of legal tender money depends directly on the Central bank. The supply of bank credits depends upon trade borrowing and so upon the lending policy of the other banks.

But the lending policy of the banks depends upon the lending policy of the Central bank. When they lend, they assume liabilities which are payable on demand in legal tender money, and they must assure themselves of adequate cash reserves to provide for these liabilities. Therefore their willingness to lend depends upon the facilities for obtaining legal tender money, and these facilities depend in turn upon the willingness of the Central bank to lend. The willingness of the Central bank to lend is measured by its " bank rate," or "rediscount rate." A variation in the rate directly affects only the other banks. But in practice they in turn usually put the rates they charge to borrowers up or down with it. Thus trade borrowing as a whole is discouraged or encouraged, and the supply of the means of payment restricted or stimulated.

This is not the place to dwell upon the mechanism of the control of credit in detail. But there is one complication so important that it must be mentioned. With a given volume of business, prices depend not only upon the quantity of the means of payment but upon its *rapidity of circulation*. Rapidity of circulation is not a very satisfactory expression, and it is not necessary to enter upon a criticism of it. What we are really concerned with is anything which tends to *increase or decrease* rapidity of circulation. And the practical form which such a tendency takes is a decreased or increased willingness on the part of the public, and especially of traders, to hold balances of money (in cash or credit). Above all, an expectation that prices will rise makes people less willing to hold such balances and an expectation that they will fall makes them more willing. When, therefore, the Central bank, by rediscounting at low rates, has once succeeded in stimulating trade borrowing, and the increase in the supply of the means of payment has started a rise in prices, the consequent increase in rapidity of circulation immediately tends to exaggerate the tendency. And *vice versa*, when high rediscount rates have checked trade borrowing, the consequent decline in rapidity of circulation exaggerate the fall of prices.

The quantity theory, enunciated, as it sometimes is, without any reference to variations in rapidity of circulation or any reservation covering such variations, is fallacious. But the principle of the regulation of the currency unit through the control of credit is not dependent on this crude form of the theory. For the changes in rapidity of circulation arising from the control of credit *reinforce* its effects. Provided the action of the Central bank is effective in accelerating or retarding trade borrowing, the resulting rise or fall of prices is greater, not less, than in proportion to the change in the quantity of means of payment. Money is not borrowed to be kept lying idle. It is paid away, as soon as borrowed, either directly, or through the medium of dealers, for the expenses of production. It is almost literally true to say that a net addition to the amount of trade borrowing in any period of time is an addition to the money income of the community for that period. The changes in the quantity of the means of payment are subsequent and consequent.

Now it is money income, not the quantity of the means of payment, that affects demand. Or rather it is money income that determines expenditure, expenditure that determines demand, demand that determines prices. Therefore the problem of regulating prices is reduced to the problem of regulating trade borrowing.

Even the power of the Central bank to regulate trade borrowing is sometimes contested. Interest on bank advances or discount on bills forms an almost negligible item in the total cost of production. Can it be supposed that an increase of 2 or 3 per cent. ($\frac{1}{2}$ to $\frac{3}{4}$ per cent. for three months) will seriously affect the willingness of producers to borrow? And even if it be admitted that experience proved the sensitiveness of business to bank rate under pre-war conditions, was not this sensitiveness largely psychological? Did not traders take the advance in bank rate as a sign of the anxiety of the Central bank, and its fears of an approaching exhaustion of its reserves?

Before the war the credit policy of Central banks was always based (as it still ostensibly is) upon the amount or proportion of gold reserves. A shortage or threatened shortage of gold reserves might be interpreted as endangering credit. The rise in the bank rate might be a danger signal, leading all lenders to fear default on the part of borrowers and to restrict operations.

But when paper money is used, a general default of borrowers on account of a shortage of cash becomes impossible. Whatever legal limitations may be imposed on the note issue cannot be maintained when the pinch comes. They could only be maintained through a refusal by the Central bank to lend after they have been reached. It is well understood that such a refusal would be fatal, and in practice it is never resorted to. (A general refusal to lend was, it is true, a characteristic of pre-war American crises, but that was in a banking system with no Central bank and no discount market.)

Nor is it in the least necessary to drag in a general fear of default from shortage of cash as the explanation of the sensitiveness of business to the bank rate or rediscount rate. It is perfectly true that the producer is not much troubled by the rate of interest he has to pay his banker. But that is not so in the case of the merchant or dealer, who is constantly carrying stocks of goods large in proportion to his own capital, and makes very nice calculations as to his margin of profit and the cost of borrowing. A moderate rise in the cost of borrowing will make the carrying of stocks appreciably less attractive to him. He will buy less and sell more, and so a fall of prices can be started.

General price variations are closely identified with the trade cycle, interest in which has lately been revived by the great trade fluctuation of the past three years. Active trade is accompanied by rising prices, that is to say by a depreciating currency unit, and depressed trade by falling prices, or an appreciating unit. Which is cause, and which is effect? Various attempts have been made to show that the trade cycle is explicable by some deep-seated non-monetary cause, and that the price variations are merely symptomatic.

There are two principal theories. One traces the trade cycle to periodical over-production, the other to periodical states of over-confidence.

According to the former, if at any time trade is active, people are tempted to invest too much money in extending the means of production. The process of investment takes time, and, as it progresses, output is gradually swollen, till it outstrips demand. Excess supply then depresses prices and discourages investment, till supply falls off, prices recover, and the cycle begins again.

According to the other theory, the root cause of the trade cycle is a long-period change in the state of business confidence. A rise or fall in confidence is contagious, and, once started, markets cannot free themselves from it till it runs up against some physical obstacle in the state of production.

The two theories are not mutually exclusive, and are usually combined, the over-investment being attributed to the over-confidence. Nor are monetary causes altogether ruled out. It is admitted that the over-confidence leads to too much trade borrowing, and so to an inflation of the means of payment.

If these theories of the trade cycle are correct, is it not vain to hope that prices can be steadied? Is it not impossible for a Central bank to alter the conditions of production or of supply and demand, or to correct the weaknesses of mob psychology?

I believe not. And I shall not stop to argue (what I believe to be true) that the trade cycle is a *purely* monetary phenomenon. Let the non-monetary theories be admitted. What then can be done by means of the control of credit?

Assume a state of over-confidence. "Confidence" here means an expectation that prices will rise, that and nothing else. To be pedantically correct, it is better to say that it means an expectation that effective demand at a given price will grow. "General business confidence" means an expectation that the effective demand for *all* commodities will grow. This expectation makes trade borrowing for the purchase of commodities attractive, and if unchecked the increase in trade borrowing will itself bring about the anticipated rise of prices. But, then, if only the cost of trade borrowing be raised high enough, its attractiveness can be counteracted. If the over-confidence does not lead to increased trade borrowing, the expectation of increased demand will be disappointed, and prices will not rise. How long the over-confidence will survive its disappointment is another matter. So long as it does survive, borrowing must be kept in check. But whether the continuance of the treatment be long or short, it will prevent a rise of prices, that is to say, a depreciation of the currency unit. In reality, of course, the over-confidence would not outlast its disappointment long. Bank rate *might* theoretically have to be raised very high to have this effect, but experience teaches that borrowing reacts to a very moderate rise.

The other branch of the problem, the counteracting of a loss of confidence, is not quite so certainly soluble. " Loss of confidence " means an expectation that prices will fall, or that demand will contract. It is theoretically conceivable in such a case that no rate of interest, however low, would tempt dealers to buy goods. Even lending money without interest would not help, if the borrower anticipated a loss on every conceivable use that he could make of the money. Business got into something very like this state in England after the American crisis of 1893. Bank rate was kept at 2 per cent. for upwards of two years before a revival began, and the open market rate for three months' bills fell below 1 per cent.

But such a condition of stagnation is not possible except in the course of reaction from a riot of inflation. If the inflation is prevented, the stagnation will never arise.

But even granted that variations in business confidence can be counteracted, how can we deal with periodical over-production? According to this theory the over-production is the result of past over-investment, which in turn is brought about by an expectation of high profits at a time of short supply. The expectation of high profits can be kept within bounds by a high rate of interest just as easily when it is due to a real shortage of stocks of commodities as when it is merely a vagary of mob psychology. What is required is to counter-act, or at any rate, to check the general desire of merchants to restore their stocks to normal. In 1919, when stocks had been nearly everywhere depleted by war conditions, a high rate on trade borrowing would have done much to guard against the danger of inflation, at all events in those countries where Government finance was not in extreme disorder.

This state of things was abnormal. It is by no means true

that under pre-war conditions a revival of trade synchronised with a shortage of stocks or a falling off with a glut. But it is not necessary to argue that point; it is enough to say that, if the shortage or the glut did occur, its effects upon prices and therefore upon profits, and therefore upon investment, could be counteracted through the instrumentality of the control of credit.

In short, whatever other factors affect the purchasing power of the monetary unit, one, the volume of trade borrowing, is amenable to human control. By its means the agency which exercises the control, that is to say, the Central bank, can correct the effects of all the others.

That does not completely dispose of all doubts as to the practicability of stabilisation. It would be vain to ignore the many difficulties in the way of the detailed application of the policy. How is the purchasing power of the unit to be measured? Any available index number is bound to be affected by price variations in particular commodities arising from non-monetary causes, such as harvest conditions, new inventions, discovery or development of new sources of supply or exhaustion of those that exist. A blind adherence to the index may hide a real departure from the path of stabilisation. And, what is almost more fundamental, a change in the monetary supply may manifest itself at first not in a change of prices at all but in a change in the volume of purchases; it may have made material progress before the index number is affected. Stabilisation cannot be secured by any hard and fast rules. The Central banks must exercise discretion; they must be ready to detect and forestall any monetary disturbance even before it has affected prices. The policy can only be perfected by long experience. Nor can it be assumed that perfect stabilisation of internal purchasing power is always reconcilable with perfect stabilisation of the foreign exchanges. The maintenance of the exchanges within a small fraction of parity, which is of the essence of the scheme, may involve a small departure of the internal purchasing power of the unit from the norm in one or more countries. A suitable compromise must be arrived at by the Central banks among themselves, but it is no use to under-estimate the difficulty of preserving an even course under such conditions.

Finally, it may be asked what real benefit a policy of direct stabilisation of the unit, even if practicable, will confer upon us. It may be freely granted that any *large* fluctuations in the commodity value of the unit, such as occur in countries with "collapsed" currencies, are a deadly evil. But is there any harm in the limited fluctuations that occurred under a gold standard before the war? The maladjustment of gold reserves, referred to above, must of course be corrected. But once the gold supply is suitably distributed, why should we not get on as we did before the war, and leave index numbers of prices to amuse the theorists?

The assumption that the maladjustment of gold reserves will have been corrected is rather a large one. But there is no need to press that point. For before the war the world *did* suffer gravely from the fluctuations in the commodity value of money, moderate as those fluctuations seemed to be. It has been pointed out above that the fluctuations of the currency unit are intimately related to the trade cycle. Now the problem of unemployment, as we knew it before the war, was nothing more nor less than the problem of the trade cycle. Unemployment there might be in particular industries independently of the trade cycle. But *general* unemployment such as prevailed in 1908-9, in 1903-5, in 1892-95, in 1884-87, in 1877-79, and in many earlier periods, was invariably a symptom of the adverse phase of the trade cycle.

So long as credit is regulated with reference to reserve proportions, the trade cycle is bound to recur. The flow of legal tender money into circulation and back is one of the very tardiest consequences of a credit expansion or contraction. If the Central bank waits for this flow to affect its reserves, and sits passively looking on at an expansion or contraction gathering impetus for years before it takes any decisive action, we cannot escape from the alternations of feverish activity with depression and unemployment. If the Central bank watches, not the reserve proportion, but the aberrations of the flow of purchasing power (as measured by prices, subject to the necessary allowances) from a perfectly even course, early action will become the rule, the expansion will be checked in time and the contraction will be avoided. Expansion and reaction have been more pronounced and more injurious in the short period that has elapsed since the war than ever before. That is because the credit situation has been allowed to drift without much regard even to the old test of reserve proportions.

To attribute our present unemployment to credit contraction may seem to run counter to the prevalent opinion, which finds the cause in the collapse of Central and Eastern European currencies. But if Continental customers cannot buy British goods, that is largely on account of that very pressure to sell, which has been brought about by the credit contraction. This pressure to sell has not only reacted adversely upon production here, but has raised the value of sterling both in commodities and in foreign currencies, and has congested markets with accumulated stocks all over the world. These consequences are not more conspicuous in European markets than elsewhere, for example, in South America and the East. Nor have we really suffered materially from the low cost of production in the countries with collapsed currencies, for by the test of the volume of exports their competition is much less formidable than before the war.

It is quite superfluous to seek for other causes of depression and unemployment, when there has been so tremendous a deflation as to reduce prices by half in less than two years. The relation of business depression to falling prices is so well recognised, not merely among economists but among practical men, that it is hardly necessary to labour the point. Experience has confirmed theory scores of times.

That does not mean to say that we do not suffer through the distresses of Europe. Our loss is heavy enough, but it does not take the form of unemployment. Unemployment is due to a defect of organisation, a maladjustment of the monetary machinery. The defect can be cured, the maladjustment can be corrected.

This is all very well, it may be said, for the countries which already have healthy currencies. By taking thought, they can perhaps do even better than before the war. But that is not the urgent problem for which the Genoa Conference was called together. What help do the resolutions offer to the countries with collapsed currencies themselves? It may be quite true that their disorders are not the cause of our depression, but that does not mean that the disorders themselves are unimportant.

These disorders are due, one and all, to budget deficits. This is true without qualification. The budget deficits themselves are due to many causes. It may possibly be true in one case that no financial expedients can provide adequate resources for the expenses of Government. If so, the budget deficit is there a symptom of a more deep-seated economic malady, a real inability to attain the subsistence level. But that at any rate is exceptional. Elsewhere budget deficits have less fundamental causes. We need not examine them in detail, but we may refer in particular to the case of international indebtedness.

To international indebtedness, whether reparations or war debts, have been attributed all the currency and exchange disturbances of Europe. Those who take this view have overlooked the fact that, apart from German reparations, practically none of the debts have even begun to be paid. Even the sums paid by Germany have been moderate in comparison with the capacity of the exchange market. The real difficulty is that the debtor countries have failed to *budget* for their liabilities. The reparation payments made by Germany up to now, have been effected not by raising the money from the taxpayer to buy the necessary exchange, but by creating inflated credits. So long as this is so, the reparation difficulty is merely the budget difficulty over again.

Undoubtedly it might be that a country, which could successfully budget for the equivalent in its own currency of its foreign obligations, would fail to create the necessary export surplus, and in that event the exchange market would break down. That situation would have to be dealt with if it arose, but it has not yet arisen.

In one respect the Genoa Resolutions are really unsatisfactory. It is impossible to point to any particular time at which effect can be given to them. Not only must they wait for the balancing of budgets before they can take effect in the weaker countries. Even in the stronger they must wait for the establishment of a gold parity, whether the restoration of the old one or the adoption of a new. England and half a dozen other countries are within less than 10 per cent. of par. But no one can say for certain how long it will take to bridge the gap. Further deflation is out of the question, and all we can do is to stabilise our currency at its existing purchasing power till the redundant supplies of gold now in America have brought down the commodity value of the dollar to the corresponding level.

Some countries, whose currencies are at less than half their pre-war gold parities, are nevertheless extremely unwilling to give up the prospect of restoring them. France, Belgium, and Italy all took this attitude at Genoa. It seems to involve an almost indefinite postponement of stabilisation so far as they are concerned.

On the other hand, countries with collapsed currencies, as soon as they have surmounted their budget difficulties, and are in a position to stabilise, will have no compunction about adopting a new parity. For them the stabilisation of the healthy currencies is by no means a matter of indifference. One of the great practical difficulties in the way of currency reform in countries like Finland or Czecho-Slovakia, which have gained effective control of their credit situation, has been the rise in the commodity value of the dollar and the pound during the past two years.

PRINTED IN GREAT BRITAIN BY THE UNIVERSITY PRESS, ABERDEEN